"This is another great book from Dorita Berger, which is a must-have for every music therapist, educator and parent. Easy to read, it gives a wealth of information on the neuroscience of music, and explains the 'why's' and 'how's' of music learning. As a parent, I learned a lot myself!"

—*Aksana Kavaliova-Moussi, MMT, BMT, MTA,*
Neurologic Music Therapist

"As the parent of a teen with autism, I can say first-hand how important music has been in his life, from learning to speak to now socializing in the marching band. This book has practical tips on how to choose an instrument, find a teacher, and even keep up with practice—a must-read for anyone who wishes to expose their child to the benefits of music."

—*Angela Scarpa, Ph.D., Associate Professor*
of Psychology and Director of the Virginia Tech
Center for Autism Research, Virginia Tech, USA

kids, music 'n' autism

by the same author

Eurhythmics for Autism and Other Neurophysiologic Diagnoses
A Sensorimotor Music-Based
Treatment Approach
Dorita S. Berger
Foreword by Stephen M. Shore.
ISBN 978 1 84905 989 3
eISBN 978 0 85700 905 0

The Music Effect
Music Physiology and Clinical Applications
Daniel J. Schneck and Dorita S. Berger
Illustrated by Geoffrey Rowland
ISBN 978 1 84310 771 2
eISBN 978 1 84642 462 5

Music Therapy, Sensory Integration
and the Autistic Child
Dorita S. Berger
ISBN 978 1 84310 700 2
eISBN 978 1 84642 712 1

of related interest

Music for Special Kids
Musical Activities, Songs, Instruments
and Resources
Pamela Ott
ISBN 978 1 84905 858 2
eISBN 978 0 85700 426 0

KIDS, MUSIC 'N' AUTISM

BRINGING OUT THE MUSIC IN YOUR CHILD

Dorita S. Berger

Jessica Kingsley *Publishers*
London and Philadelphia

First published in 2017
by Jessica Kingsley Publishers
73 Collier Street
London N1 9BE, UK
and
400 Market Street, Suite 400
Philadelphia, PA 19106, USA

www.jkp.com

Copyright © Dorita S. Berger 2017

Library of Congress Cataloging in Publication Data
Names: Berger, Dorita S., author.
Title: Kids, music 'n' autism : bringing out the music in your child / Dorita
    S. Berger.
Other titles: Kids, music and autism
Description: Philadelphia ; London : Jessica Kingsley Publishers, 2017. |
    Includes bibliographical references and index.
Identifiers: LCCN 2016026946 | ISBN 9781785927164 (alk. paper)
Subjects: LCSH: Children with autism spectrum disorders--Education. |
    Music--Instruction and study. | Special education. | Music therapy for
    children.
Classification: LCC MT17 .B47 2017 | DDC 780.87--dc23 LC record available at
https://lccn.loc.gov/2016026946

British Library Cataloguing in Publication Data
A CIP catalogue record for this book is available from the British Library

ISBN 978 1 78592 716 4
eISBN 978 1 78450 314 7

Printed and bound in Great Britain

Where words fail, music speaks.
HANS CHRISTIAN ANDERSEN

I dedicate this book to every parent, caregiver, teacher, grandparent, aunt, uncle, friend, and significant persons committed to bringing increased quality of life through the wonders of music to the many children on the autism spectrum and those with other diagnoses who struggle to excel and live life to the fullest.

May music add health to your lives!

CONTENTS

Part 2: Providing Music in a Child's Life

PRELUDE

Years ago I wrote an article that was later published in a give-away parents' newspaper in New York City, that dealt with how to take children to concerts—how to prepare them for the experience, how to gather material describing the music they would be hearing, and more. It was a well-received article that subsequently motivated me to consider writing a book on the subject of "Kids 'n' Music" that could provide useful information on various other related topics on this theme. After years of teaching piano, taking school students to concerts, providing professional music-based clinical treatment for a variety of diagnosed children, and assisting parents on various "how to" issues, I outlined such a book, and it sat unnoticed in my documents file as a "someday" project.

Move forward to the year 2016, when I received a note from Jessica Kingsley Publishers that my fourth book, *Eurhythmics for Autism and Other Neuropschologic Diagnoses: A Sensorimotor Music-Based Treatment Approach*, had been released (November, 2015). I took a breath feeling very relieved, and, as a tongue-in-cheek response, I wrote my editor, Lisa Clark, attaching my "Kids 'n' Music" outline, saying, (in jest), "Okay, now I'm ready for my next book!" although I had decided that I was done writing books! It was truly meant as a joke, since I was exhausted from the production of the *Eurhythmics for Autism* book, and I knew that this publisher does not undertake mass-market publishing! Well, one must be very careful what one speaks! Lisa perused the outline, and the previously published article about taking children to concerts, and responded that she'd be very interested in publishing this book, provided I would focus it toward Autism and special needs children, applicable to JKP readership! Wow, I thought! Do I have the energy to embark on yet another book, so soon? But the idea of specifying the material towards special needs populations intrigued me, and would provide the opportunity for me to advise parents in a similar manner as I had been advising throughout my professional work. A month after my *Eurhythmics for Autism* book was released, I was in contract to write this book!

Herein is the result. So first, I would like to acknowledge and thank my talented and intuitive Jessica Kingsley editor, Lisa Clark, along with her excellent production staff, for pushing me, suggesting to me, correcting me, and for working all hours, to bring about amazing publications that benefit so many clinicians, caretakers, teachers, and interested persons raising and working with special needs populations. And, I add a loud BRAVO! to Jessica Kingsley Publishers for being recognized by the 2016 British Book Industry Awards as Independent Academic, Educational & Professional Publisher of the Year. I am honored to be on the roster of JKP authors. Thank you, Jessica Kingsley, Lisa Clark, and staff at JKP for your dedication and hard work.

While writing this book, I wanted the readers to find the material to be accessible and comfortable to read. I felt that the addition of some humorous illustrations could be fun to include. To that end, I contacted visual artist Geoffrey Rowland, art instructor and Chair of the Fine Arts Department at Auburn High School in Riner, Virginia, to suggest the possibility that some talented art students in his classes might like to contribute some illustrations as a special project for extra credits. Mr. Rowland, some readers may recall, had previously illustrated the Schneck & Berger book *The Music Effect* (JKP, 2006), so I thought he would be helpful in this respect. Mr. Rowland undertook the suggestion, and several months later I received a copy of the illustration that is now included in this book, at the beginning of Chapter 6. It is a beautifully conceived illustration rendered by a 15-year old freshman student in Mr. Rowland's art class, Miss Miriam Gallup Jones, from the Christiansburg, Virginia area. I was delighted with this student's depiction of a young person pounding on a piano to display either frustration or anger, perhaps loving the piano but hating to practice. The illustration is so delightful, and so artistically rendered by the young talented art student, that I felt it was appropriate for inclusion. So thank you, Miss Miriam G. Jones from Mr. Geoffrey Rowland's art class at Auburn High School, for your wonderful contribution, and for your excellent artistic talent! Thank you, Mr. Rowland, Miriam, and Mr. and Mrs. Jones, for giving the publishers and me permission to include this illustration. Auburn High School in Riner, Virginia, will be very proud of your achievement.

The most important person I would like to acknowledge and thank, among many others, is my singing colleague, educator, and friend in Durham, North Carolina, Marie Hammond, for volunteering to undertake the important (and very time-consuming) project of reading through the raw text, editing the Ps and Qs, commas, misspellings, grammatical inconsistencies, and general sensibility of the material, prior to my submission of the draft to the publisher. Without Marie's initial suggestions, corrections, and input, readers may have had some confusions reading the material. Marie and her wonderful pianist-husband Sam participate in the Triangle

Jewish Chorale in Durham/Chapel Hill, North Carolina. Marie sings tenor voice in the choir, and Sam accompanies, orchestrates, and participates in rehearsals and performances. The Hammonds are very special people, and I am very lucky and honored to have their friendship and support. Thank you, Marie and Sam, for your interest in my work.

Finally, to list and acknowledge the many families, parents, clients, students, musicians, professionals, and friends who have influenced the ideas and suggestions found in the following pages, would be to write another 20 pages. I will simply say *Thank you* to all, most of you know of whom I speak. Your knowledge and contribution of insights continue to stimulate my interests and professionalism, and I hope this book will pay tribute to your high standards of thinking.

ABOUT KIDS 'N' MUSIC: A LETTER TO PARENTS

Dear Parents and Caregivers,

Allow me to introduce myself and share some thoughts for you to consider as you read through this book of advice and suggestions. I'm Dr. Dorita Berger, and everyone calls me Doc Dori. I have been in music all my life. I began studying piano when I was five years old, after my mother took me to see the movie about the life of Chopin (titled *A Song to Remember*, produced by Columbia Pictures, 1945). While the story itself may or may not uphold full authenticity, the music certainly does, and is performed by Arthur Rubinstein (in the background, as actor Cornel Wilde portrays Chopin). I, even at that young age, somehow instinctively understood the emotional energy of Chopin's beautiful piano music. I soon urged my parents to schedule piano lessons for me, and continued studying and concertizing through most of my upbringing and formative years, into adulthood and onward. It never occurred to me that there were persons who were not musicians! My world-view was through music and creative expression. My self-discipline emanated from my hours of repetitive, concentrated learning and performance of music.

I hold a BFA in Piano Performance from Carnegie Mellon University (Pennsylvania), an MA in Music Therapy from NYU (New York), and a PhD in Physiologic (Sensorimotor) Music Therapy from the Psychology Department of Roehampton University (London, England). After many years of performing, I decided to apply music in a clinical manner by treating people of special needs through the many energetic elements and expressions of music, and have spent the past 20-plus years providing music-based treatment services and/or piano lessons to persons on the autism spectrum, among others, of all ages, abilities, and walks of life. During the years as a music-based clinician, I have engaged in a wide variety of music interactions with diagnosed youngsters, from teaching adaptive piano to using music, rhythm, and movement (eurhythmics) for sensory motor adaptation, and have observed phenomenal results derived from experience with music. Throughout my professional life, I have been asked many questions by parents, teachers, and caregivers about music for their child. This led me to consider writing this book that may provide some answer to questions asked.

Why am I writing this letter to you before writing the rest of this book? Because knowing my background may help you, the reader, gain trust in the information you will be reading, and in the suggestions and recommendations I will be sharing with you. I, too, have raised children, and now enjoy observing my grandchildren grow. Although my daughters were never diagnosed with ASD, they each had "special needs" in some manner, whether artistically gifted, special learning styles, high energy, stress, anxiety, and more. I believe all youngsters, in one way or another, have "special needs," whether or not such has been officially diagnosed. I understand parenting a child with "special" skills and alternative behaviors, whether driven by talent or by psycho-emotional or physiological urgency. And all children—whether diagnosed or not—are drawn towards interacting with music, and in many instances indeed are musically brilliant, and capable of studying instrumental skills. Yes, problems most probably arise more frequently with diagnosed children: frustrations; sensory and physical difficulties; inattentiveness; cognitive delays; behavioral anxieties; and much more. However, these issues are *not* unique to diagnosed children, but rather may be seen in every growing child experiencing many of the characteristics designated to autism! That is why I am asking that you think beyond the "spectrum"—because not all childhood behaviors are the result of a diagnosis! There are individual personality characteristics at play—and much of the information within this book can apply to *any* child.

I look forward to sharing with you advice and recommendations, and hope that the information will be helpful to you, your child or children, and their interaction with music. I will not encumber you with references. We are all capable of searching the internet for supportive information to validate or further illuminate information. I will leave that up to you. There are inexhaustible amounts of books and literature on any subject related to ASD, music activities, etc. Herein I am not providing a recipe book of "activities" *per se*, but rather I would like to encourage you and suggest ways to include music in the development of your diagnosed child, and to have the courage to believe that indeed, music has a role to play in your child's development—whether or not the child is diagnosed.

What you will read is based on my experiences as a parent, a musician, a performer, a clinician—and as an author who can relay useful information for the betterment and wellbeing of your child.

Thank you for your kind attention.

Doc Dori
Dorita S. Berger, PhD, LCAT, MT-BC

MUSIC IS IMPORTANT FOR THE DEVELOPING CHILD

CHAPTER 1

HOW AND WHY TO THINK BEYOND THE SPECTRUM

I would teach children music, physics, and philosophy; but most importantly music, for the patterns in music and all the arts are the key to learning.

PLATO

Why music?

Answer: *Why not?* Everyone loves music! It exists everywhere in every culture on the planet. Apparently, human brains are wired to process music. Music is a whole-brain-whole-body experience. Music is essential for growth and development of children of *all* abilities and *any* function. "Music and the brain" has been a hot topic of research and discussion for the past several decades. My friend and colleague, neuroscientist (and saxophone player) Dr. Nina Kraus, of the BrainVolts lab at Northwestern University in Chicago, Illinois[1] informs us that the brains of persons who have had musical and instrumental training function at a more efficient

---

1   www.brainvolts.northwestern.edu

level than the brains of those who have had little or no musical training in formative years. Dr. Kraus and many other researchers around the world have identified music as a major contributor to brain development, cognition, and physiological function. This includes its effectiveness in *diagnosed* persons as well! There is also extensive scientific research discovering that music training in early life may also delay, or even inhibit, the onset of various dementias in later years.

That music activities have positive impact on child development, including sensory, cognitive, language, movement, and social skills development, is now considered to be a given. Surfing on the internet provides an abundance of researched, documented, and generally accepted journal articles attesting to the positive contribution of music to the growing special-needs child on the autism spectrum, and children with other diagnoses. The clinical field of music therapy defines and describes evidence-based treatments servicing many diagnoses with resulting effectiveness. All of this has led to unlimited numbers of advice-seeking parents searching for information on issues related to accessing music activities, instrumental-skills training, and/or clinical music-based services for their special child.

In order to help a special-needs child enter and become part of the music culture in which he or she lives, it is helpful for parents, caregivers, teachers, aides, and family members to understand and repeat an important mantra: *A diagnosis does NOT pre-empt talent!* What's more, one needs to eliminate the word "savant," and move *beyond* diagnoses. I have not heard the term "savant" applied to a typically functioning child who, at the age of four, happens to be a musical prodigy, or a scientific or mathematical "genius." I have mostly heard the word "savant" used in relation to autism, and I am often put off by that. We are *all* savants in one form or other, whether as cooks, authors, scientists, or just parents. So in effect, perhaps we are all "on the spectrum"!

Indeed, we need to think beyond the "spectrum" and instead investigate the *abilities* of a child, rather than focusing on *dis*-abling limitations, and being shocked when abilities are displayed! In actuality, there are no such things as "*dis*abilities"—but rather "*in*abilities" in some ways of functioning within "typically expected" manners, therefore necessitating access to *alternative* abilities and possibilities. This pertains to *any* diagnoses. Exemplifying this concept is none other than the world-renowned physicist Professor Stephen Hawking, whose brilliant brain and mind happen to reside in a completely incapacitated physical structure called "body."

As far as music is concerned, in its presence *no one is unable*—everyone is equal! There are no *dis*abilities in the presence of this predominantly non-verbal aesthetic form of self-expression! There is only *ability*. An example of this is the musician Evelyn Glennie, the world-famous concert percussionist who happens to be profoundly deaf. Her lack of auditory function has not stopped her from studying music, an acoustic art form in which hearing would seem to be crucial to her career. Instead, Ms. Glennie has adapted to "hearing" through her body.[2] In other words, as Ms. Glennie suggests, there are no *dis*abilities, but rather, certain limitations that can be resolved in many alternative ways through certain required adaptations, whether by technology or assistive personnel. Music activities address *abilities*, and are immensely

---

2   www.evelyn.co.uk

useful in bringing about creativity, self-awareness, stress reduction, physical and sensory coordination, social skills, and a sense of belonging and mindful wellbeing. It is a unique interface with child development that truly enhances brain development!

Music makes good sense

Throughout the years of my professional life, I have been asked for advice by parents, teachers, and administrators on how to address certain aspects involving special-needs children and music activities, questions covering the whole gamut: at what age to begin introducing music; what activities to do at home; what kind of music to listen to; how music induces language development; if and when to begin music training; how to select appropriate instruments; what to do about instrumental practice habits and regulation if the child has behavior issues; how to prepare and take special-needs children to concerts; what is music therapy vs. music lessons; and whether the child is "teachable." I have also been asked to attend school meetings regarding the child and school music classes.

In essence, as stated earlier, a diagnosis does not pre-empt talent and creativity, and not all behaviors and observed characteristics are consequences of a diagnosis! This is an erroneous assumption held by many persons. In fact, every child has innate personality characteristics that often are *not* commensurate with a diagnosis. There is a complete independent person inside that body, DNA- and heredity-driven! Stubborn is as stubborn does! Anxious is as anxious does! Creative is as creative does. And so on. Indeed, separating personality traits from diagnosis-related characteristics is often difficult and confusing for family members. The tendency is to attribute behaviors to a diagnosis: *Ah, so that's what is the problem—autism* (or ADHD, etc.). It is as if having a diagnosis can explain everything. Not so! Enter music. Music can separate the diagnosed *label* from the *persona*. Music is the perfect medium for shedding light on *who* the child is, from inside out.

Despite science, medicine and research interests in music, the brain, and child development, there has been very little written to advise parents, caregivers, educators and teachers, schools, as well as the general public, regarding helpful approaches in support and acceptance of the need for music interactions in alternative management and skills development of children on the autism spectrum, and *all* children, for that matter. In this book, I seek to present easy-to-read, often light-hearted and amusingly accessible discussions of typical and non-typical circumstances involving special kids 'n' music. I hope to answer some of your questions and to inspire and encourage you, the reader, to infuse your child's life with music.

Quick overview of this book

Kids, Music 'n' Autism is meant to be an easy reader answering some questions that parents have asked me over the years, regarding music and their child. The book is organized into three sections, each including various chapters that are complete and informative in themselves, requiring no previous associative information. Reading the chapters in sequence is not necessary, although it is recommended in order to accumulate information validating the suggested urgency to include music in every child's life, why and how, regardless of diagnoses, abilities, and interests. However, chapters are independent of each other, and may be selected according to interests.

The main section of the book opens, as you may have already seen, with an *Overture* "About Kids 'n' Music: A Letter to Parents." sharing some of my own professional background as a musician and music-based clinician, and some of my beliefs about the need to bring music to every child, and especially children on the autism spectrum and those with various other diagnoses.

Part One: These first three chapters in Part One ask the reader to think beyond the spectrum, and to focus more on the abilities of the diagnosed child, rather than disabilities. These chapters discuss music and the sensory systems; the "musical brain;" why music makes "good sense;" how sensory systems, language and cognition respond to music; creating music with found objects; and general (simple) information on issues related to music activities for a child with special needs, both in the home and outside. Included are suggestions on types of CDs that make sense for various activities, ages, and interests, when to have music in the background (e.g., at meal times, bedtime, relaxation time), and so on.

Chapters 2 and 3 briefly discuss the sensory systems critical to functional behaviors, and some physiological and cognitive reasons for including music as a *lifelong* part of development and continuity for a child on the autism spectrum, and also for children with other diagnoses, as well as for typically functioning children. In these chapters the reader will gain information drawn from current research in music and language, music and brain, music and rhythm internalization for movement and coordination, music for stress-release (yes, even children have stress!), music for cognitive development, music therapy and social skills, and like concerns. I do not provide references or links to this information, in order not to encumber the reader's reading momentum, but I urge readers to research articles and information of interest for themselves, for "proof" of the importance of music in development. I myself have written several academic books and articles on music in human adaptation and autism spectrum populations, which contain extensive bibliographies and research citations.[3] In addition to my books, many other clinicians and researchers have authored professional books for music therapy professionals, and for music, science, and brain researchers, that are available through several book-purchasing locations online (e.g., Amazon).

Part Two: This section generally explores and discusses a multitude of topics directly related to kids 'n' music. Chapters in this section provide suggestions about selecting appropriate instruments for skills training; how to find a music teacher and/or music therapist; how to manage instrumental practice; how to prepare and take children to live concerts and what behaviors to expect; how to advocate for the child in public; and other information that readers may find useful. Chapter 4 discusses exploring music lessons vs. music therapy; highlights information about eurhythmics movement training; gives advice on how to locate and interview instrumental or vocal instructors for training the child on the spectrum and other special needs; and examines whether music therapy might be a better option with which to begin musical skills learning.

---

3   Readers can investigate my publications and articles at www.academia.edu and/or the Jessica Kingsley Publishers website (www.jkp.com), where much information on music and autism can be found.

Chapter 5 discusses things to consider when choosing and selecting particular instrument(s) to learn, depending on the age of the child; where and how to begin; studying the piano, stringed instruments, brass and wind instruments, drums, or guitar. Chapter 6 discusses some of the issues that often arise with the need to practice an instrument: whether to force; parental role; expectations and attitudes; commitment and consistency; schedules; thoughts and recommendations. Chapter 7 raises the many potential problems of taking a child to public concerts. This chapter suggests ways to prepare children in advance before attending live concert experiences; for instance, where to sit in the venue, how long a time to remain at a concert, what is or is not appropriate behavior in general, what to expect and accept from the child, and various additional concerns.

Part Three: The concluding two chapters discuss various additional things to think about, and provide some resources for locating music therapists, and Dalcroze Eurhythmics organizations internationally. Chapter 8 discusses the future of the musically gifted diagnosed child; children with exceptional obstacles that can interfere with music learning, such as auditory and visual sensitivities; the pros and cons of using earphones; considerations for deaf or blind music students; music and arousal behaviors. Chapter 9 begins with a brief look at brain development to further give emphasis to the importance of including music for a developing child from birth onward, regardless of whether there is or there is not a diagnosis. This chapter also offers concluding thoughts, and provides an international listing of music therapy organizations around the world, including several Dalcroze Eurhythmics Centers for obtaining further information and attainment of specialists in music therapy and eurhythmics movement.

The *Finale* comes full circle with final quotes by Plato and by the late Dr. Oliver Sacks. The reader is asked not to consider this book as a "technical" book, or a diagnostic book describing various attributes of autism or other physiological functions. Instead, the main objective in writing this book is to encourage and support the idea that *music should be in every child's life*, from the beginning of life, throughout life, at all levels of abilities, whether or not a child is diagnosed!

Music is an equalizer. There are no *dis*abilities when encountering music.

Formal or informal interactions—at home, in schools, in music lessons, in music therapy—are equal contributors to the wellbeing of any child! As stated earlier, this book seeks to respond to various questions that arise in day-to-day, practical concerns regarding music and special-needs children, providing ideas, suggestions, and advice on how to think about certain things in relation to autism and music, and how and where to obtain internet information and research papers for scientific "proof" about music, the brain, and child development. This book should be easy to read and informative for parents and others who may want better to understand music's impact on human behavior and adaptation.

In all, it is hoped that many questions will have found answers, and that music will, indeed, become a standard part of every child's life!

CHAPTER 2

THE *SENSE-ABILITY* OF THE MUSICAL BRAIN

Music is the mediator between the life of the senses and the life of the spirit.

LUDWIG VAN BEETHOVEN

Music and sensory education from the beginning

Dear reader, this chapter will be a bit more complex, and may require a little more cognitive power, so grab a cup of coffee, sit back, relax, and allow your sensory systems to "chill out" while your brain does the thinking. In essence, you will come to appreciate that music should be part of every child's health and education formula, from the beginning. Why? Because *music is a whole-brain-whole-body experience* that can address physiological, cognitive, and emotional function without the need to know anything about music! Music does not require language or semantic understanding in order to impact sensory, physiological, cognitive, and emotional systems.

Music is energy—an energy that vibrates in the form of organized sound. Those vibrations massage the body, in a sense, contributing to the brain's sense of body. The external auditory inputs develop the brain's rhythmically organized neuronal interactions, ultimately organizing for a "better brain", according to neuroscience research. Why do parents sing or cue lullaby music to calm a child? It is because music can soothe to keep the brain from functioning in an anxious state. The sooner the system can attain an anxiety-free state, the sooner that sensory systems can coordinate, the more likely it will be that the brain will learn functionally adaptive modulation from anxiety to calm. Let us start from the beginning and investigate a little physiology and the sensory systems, because so many types of diagnoses, from autism, ADHD, Down syndrome, etc. to Alzheimer's, present sensory problems, whether visual, auditory, or gross or fine motor inefficiencies, often leading to various behavioral disruptions.

Music and the vestibular and proprioceptive senses

We are all born with an abundance of sensory systems ready to tackle survival. The first thing a newborn's brain has to battle is gravity! And for managing gravity, the brain must know where the body is and what it is doing relative to the g-force—gravitational stress—and space. After comfortably floating in the womb's amniotic fluid, baby's home for nine months, the baby's brain immediately must activate the *vestibular system* (balance), integrating with the *proprioception system* (muscle and joint activities), to inform the brain of where the body is in space, what it is doing, and in what position are its muscles and joints. Out of the womb, the brain has to manage this g-force to determine what is up or down, top or bottom, in order to confirm its position in space. In many birthing cases, one may notice that the newborn's first physical reaction to having just been plucked from the womb is to stiffen and thrust its arms upward, palms open, as if trying to reach for something that will keep the body from falling. Already, survival-anxiety takes hold! That response is an instinctive corrective maneuver that is practiced and repeated for the rest of any person's life—a kind of reaching for and correcting balance—for evermore! Just the act of walking, for instance, is a fall and rebound, the brain needing rhythmically to gauge precisely when the second leg will come forth to "catch" the body as it leans forward. We take these actions for granted because they have become instinctive, after being practiced from the age of some nine months.

Then there are all the other sensations introduced to the newborn for the first time. The newborn as yet knows nothing of the planet, but in addition to gravity, that brain is already dealing with light (visual), sound (auditory), tactile sensations (being touched by various attendants, being washed, sensing the body being cold or warm, etc.), physical (proprioceptive/vestibular) sensory information, taste (breast or bottle, milk or formula), and the multitude of scents (smell of the mother, hospital ward, nurses, and more). These are primary survival sensory system instincts at play, some before, but most after being pulled onto this planet. Bottom line: the brain's information of environmental conditions, both internal and external, comes only from the sensory systems. Thus, from the beginning, it is important that the sensory systems develop well in order to transmit information accurately, to be well perceived by the brain.

How does music interact with the vestibular and proprioceptive systems? First, the vestibular system involves the head and ears. The auditory nerve affects the vestibular system. Without going into all the details easily obtainable elsewhere, suffice it to say that vestibular balance involves head positions and the flow of fluid within the ear canal that will ultimately determine the position of the body in relation to the position of the head. Cilia (hair-like structures) located on one side of the two-sided cochleas canal (a spiral structure like a shell) in the inner ear are disturbed and transmit electric signals that eventually reach the brain and are translated as elements of sound. The vestibular flow of fluid uses the other side of this canal, so it can influence the sound-receiving side, in some manner, and vice versa. A person with inefficient hearing will often complain of loss of balance. Research suggests that one's sense of rhythm perception is somewhat related to vestibular function.

All quite complex, but to put it simply, auditory and vestibular sensory systems interact within the same apartment house, and each can potentially be regulated from birth. Additionally, because the auditory and the motor cortexes in the brain are very close to each other, music's rhythm implicates movement, which in turn stimulates muscular motor activities (foot tapping, clapping, dancing). Such responses rely on the brain knowing (we hope) the precise position of its body (muscle and joints) after assessing information received from the proprioception system. This processing of information is instinctive and automatic. Instigating movement from the beginning of life can later assist with better muscle tone for balance and vestibular function. It is quite likely that with the inclusion of music from the beginning of a child's life, perhaps sensory integration problems involving auditory, proprioceptive, and vestibular systems, could be forestalled, or at least minimized, even before a diagnosis of ASD or ADHD or other syndromes evolve. A long shot? Perhaps, but why not consider it? There is so much research yet to be undertaken! At the very least, music can help to strengthen sensory function, and later to control movement.

In addition to balance, as stated earlier, the brain needs to know about the container in which it resides—its body! As many parents with diagnosed children know, proprioception tells the brain about the body—about its limbs, positions, states of muscle contractions, joints, and internal organs, and what these are doing at any given instance. This information enables the brain to know about the container in which it resides—"the self"—where this self begins and ends, when the self needs to be fed, to sleep, to be held firmly secured by parent, bed, chair, so that it will not float in the air (as it floated in the womb) and fall. Proprioception also helps the brain know where the body's limbs are, and in what position. In short, proprioception is responsible for enabling any and all movement. Living creatures, including humans, never stop determining what's up from what's down.

Music activities with the infant provide proprioceptive input to the brain. First, the energy vibration transmitted from musical instruments and timbre, provides proprioceptive input from outside of the body, enveloping the body, helping the brain to map its body's perimeter. In order to play drums, or lift a pencil, the brain must first know the position of the body and limbs, because this action requires grasping of mallets (or pencil), lifting arms, applying specific muscular force to hold the mallets and to strike the instrument—actions requiring feedback/feedforward interaction between the brain, the nervous system, and it's body parts. Proprioception, uniting with the vestibular, results in developing muscle tone, which is often lacking in spectrum and other diagnosed children. Music activity instigates various instinctive responses, and added to these a sense of *self*-awareness and awareness of "other."

Music and the auditory, visual, and tactile systems

Needless to point out, music activities address systems *collectively*, not one at a time. We *feel/ hear/see* how we and others make music, we *see/touch* (and taste, if wind instrument) the instruments or mallets, we *see/touch/smell* the resin on the bow, our senses interacting instinctively and simultaneously. In addition, there are inner brain rhythms to sensory system processing of information, all happening collaboratively. If there is something amiss in sensory processing, then the more that music activity is presented, the more such collaborations can be better organized to become adaptive, automatically! There can never be too much interaction between a child *of any age and function*, and music! It is a highly noninvasive way to address sensory and cognitive development, calmness, attention, eye contact, motor regulation, sequential auditory and visual processing, language development, and much more.

There is no better way to address and to develop adaptive auditory processing, crucial to language development, than through the interaction of the system with music. Research has determined that the auditory system is one of the first (if not the first) to develop *in utero*, so by the time the newborn enters the world, sound is already familiar to the brain. Appropriate auditory function is critical for survival! Auditory sound location, sound discrimination (timbre and pitch differentiation), can make the difference between life and death! After all, one must surely identify a sound's pitch and timbre as being that of a lion and not a puppy dog, and that the lion may be too close for comfort! In pregnancy, some women have reported sensing the fetus actually kicking in rhythm to external music being heard. Already, a sense of motor response and sound discrimination is being practiced. Science researchers have concluded that a newborn can recognize its mother's voice compared with the voices of other women, and can also discriminate timbres between male and female voices. Toddlers aged two and three years also seem able to discriminate dissonant vs. consonant music, already displaying likes and dislikes—musical taste! These findings have been replicated in research at various institutions throughout the world. The BrainVolts Lab at Northwestern University in Chicago[4] has presented new research suggesting that any and all sounds to which the brain is exposed, beginning in infancy and perhaps even before, will shape how the brain and auditory systems will ultimately process future sound input, and indicating how this finding may implicate later perception of language sounds, as well as music perception.

A note about auditory and visual processing for survival: The questions comes up *What about sensory survival needs of persons with profound hearing and/or visual deficits?* The fact is, if one or more sensory systems are inactive, for whatever reasons, other systems take over. The tactile system responds to vibrations set off by sounds. One "hears" throughout the body, and ultimately learns to discriminate various timbres and volume (louds and softs) that signify safety or danger. If sight is lacking, the auditory

---

4   www.brainvolts.northwestern.edu

and tactile systems will compensate; if auditory is lacking, the visual and tactile systems will validate the environment; if both are lacking, then touch (the tactile) and smell (olfactory) systems become all the more hypervigilant. Research indicates that if a blind person touches an item, the occipital lobe responsible for vision processing in the brain actually activates, despite not receiving visual information! The tactile sense is the major survival-enabling sensory system, along with taste and smell. In short, the brain will use whichever system can aid in determining safety from danger. In essence, the whole body "hears" sound! This factor further supports the need for music activities to sensitize the body and sensory systems further.

Music and anxiety reduction

Music soothes. We all know this! But how? Very simply, music goes straight into the subcortical areas of the brain, including the thalamus, hypothalamus, and best of all, the amygdala! This little brain organ, the size of an almond, is, by many, considered to be the "emotional" part of the inner brain. All sensory information coming into the brain is "interviewed" to determine whether the information is safe, or whether it presents a threat to survival of the system! The amygdala is associated, by some, to be the "fear" center of the brain. This means that if the hypothalamus (sensory processing) and the amygdala together determine that some incoming information is dangerous, chemicals called catecholamines immediately begin to be excreted, to prepare the system for fight or flight. Some catecholamines we are all familiar with include adrenalin and cortisone, among many others! Safety and survival depend on what is known to function as the hypothalamus-pituitary-adrenal (HPA) axis. The hypothalamus produces catecholamines, sends them down to be stored in the pituitary and adrenal glands, to be released at the sign of danger! Now, the actions of the HPA is temporary, and things are back to "normal" once the danger has seemingly passed. However, there are many diagnosed populations whose HPA axes are hyperactive, releasing adrenalin and cortisone more continuously, even when there is no danger. This is a state of anxiety and an overactive amygdala seeing danger everywhere, mostly imagined!

Music pacifies and quiets the amygdala! In doing so, the "survival-anxiety" axis is called off, and the body goes into nice, relaxed, quiet behavior. This event is precisely what many diagnosed populations require, because autism and other diagnoses live in a constant state of anxiety and fear! And music meets that challenge. From birth. This is how your lullaby pacifies your baby. This is how rhythm, movement, music-making, and listening calms everyone's system—automatically! We cannot say "calm down" to ourselves or others, because, as we all know, words do not do the trick. But putting on a nice CD of music one enjoys, will distract the brain from its anxieties, reduce the flow of cortisol and adrenalin, and relax the mind–body.

This is, perhaps, the main *sense*-ability of music! This is how the sensory systems can attain positive interactions, because once the brain no longer has to be concerned with "survival," it can devote attention to other processes, including cognition, memory, and learning. Be aware that as long as the brain is concerned with fight-flight survival, the memory organ in the brain—the hippocampus—shuts down, inhibiting memory and retention of learned information! This is why a spectrum child has difficulty learning. That system is in a constant state of survival anxiety—

fear—to the extent that cognition shuts down, fight-flight takes over with melt-downs and erratic behaviors. Music—particularly rhythm—can redirect this! Music is motivating. Music distracts the mind. Music is enjoyable. Music is calming. Music needs to be part of every day's sensory diet, for anyone, at any age—but especially for developing children, on or off the spectrum. All children are anxious. Growing up is frightening. Seeking constant adult approval is tiring. Learning new behaviors—even learning to walk and falling—is stressful.

Enough physiology! Music is sensible—period. Music is *sense*-able. Readers can learn more about music and human function, the sensory systems, the brain, and related topics, if motivated, by reading some of my other books, along with a multitude of books, articles and papers of others found online. No need to encumber this chapter with more technical information. You've probably finished your coffee and I prefer to move into other chapters to suggest some age-appropriate music, and how to include music on behalf of child development, and other useful information.

CHAPTER 3

MUSIC FOR ALL AGES AND ANY FUNCTION

Music is the shorthand of emotion.

LEO TOLSTOY

In our Chapter 2 discussion of music and the sensory systems, I clearly advocated for the incorporation of music into a child's everyday life, daily, from birth (and even *in utero*). We considered the role of music interaction with sensory systems, because sensory coordination and integration are so often problematic in spectrum and otherwise diagnosed children of all ages. In this chapter we continue the discussion, sharing thoughts and recommendations for having music on a daily basis, and for various reasons.

We are at a time when music and brain research is ongoing, with unusual discoveries of how the brain regulates and processes information. Language processing in the brain has been extensively researched over the centuries. The role of music in human adaptation is taking the stage. Music is everywhere, daily, changing moods, energies, thoughts, feelings, concentration, and keeping us company in daily activities. Most important is the role of music in emotion regulation, beginning at birth. For several centuries scientists have been discussing the importance of regulating emotions, starting in infancy and continuing through toddler ages, in order to assure the development of good emotional function in adulthood. Online searches will produce many journal papers by important 19th century scientists, such as William James, and more currently Dr. Sandra Trehub, Dr. Laurel J. Trainor, and others too numerous to list, discussing emotional development in the very young, and the contribution of music to such emotional regulation. (Tags for searches: music and babies; music in child development.)

As Tolstoy suggests in the quotation at the start of this chapter, music speaks *about*, and *to*, human emotions. Music not only includes emotional energies within itself, but also draws from, and reflects emotional sensations from the performer, and from the listener. Earlier we learned that music requires no semantic explanations. Music is, indeed, a "shorthand" expression of feelings. Music *is* emotion, and it reaches directly into the emotional processing areas of the brain.

Chapter 2 also informed readers that music can quiet the hypothalamic-pituitary-adrenal (HPA) axis, to reduce anxieties and to calm the system. For these and many other reasons, music ought to be part of the environment of any home and family, even in the background for much of the day, as is oxygen in the air, from the very start of life. All early intervention programs for diagnosed youngsters ought to include music/movement activities, preferably more active music making (even infants can be prompted to beat a drum, feel a tambourine, move legs, etc.) in addition to passive music listening. Let us take a look a various age groups and how music can successfully interact with various activities. The following are some recommendations to consider.

Birth to six: Music for the developing emotional brain

These formative years set the foundations for further physical and emotional regulation. In special-needs children, most diagnoses are not provided until the child reaches the age of two, and sometimes earlier if the child is born with particular deficits such as brain traumas, missing limbs and senses, and other birth shortcomings. For the most part, signs of possible problems evolve slowly. Even when being unaware that something could be amiss, music should be incorporated *from the beginning of a child's life*. From birth the child needs to learn to "feel good" inside of his or her own body, and outside with the world at large. Music helps with emotion regulation and development, as well as physiological coordination. As suggested earlier, it may be possible that just having music around might slow oncoming symptoms of a later-discovered diagnosis. So for this age group, consider the advice and recommendations in the following sections.

Sleep time
Whether nap or night sleep, pre-recorded slow, quiet, *instrumental* lullaby songs work best, unless a parent prefers to sing. Objectives are to keep the brain and body calm, relaxed, and sleepy, without providing too much auditory/cognitive information that the brain has to process. My preference is the use of recorded instrumental lullabies rather than tingling artificial music-box type of tunes

played by less "natural" means. Beautifully recorded music played on acoustic instruments or voice is recommended. (Actually, one never outgrows the need for beautiful music to induce sleep.) Rocking, of course, calms the system, and parent singing (provided that Mom or Dad has good pitch and a soothing voice) is lovely. This suggestion is not new to any caregiver, of course. The important issue here is to find recordings of acoustic instrumental tunes, and that may be difficult in these days of digital electronic reproduction. Acoustic instruments are "natural" instruments, not electronic. This means the use of a real piano, violins, etc., played by live performers, rather than digitally reproduced by a computer. Piano music such as Chopin Nocturnes, or that of Debussy, Ravel and other Impressionist composers, and slow movements of various chamber music compositions (Haydn and Mozart Quartets, and Baroque era music, for instance), and less boisterous movements of symphonic works from the Classical and Romantic music era— in other words, original works, rather than anything simulated and contrived to simulate various genres of music. Exposure to "authentic" works can also develop good music taste for the child!

Recommendation: Although I usually refrain for suggesting particular music works, I would like to share some advice. First, music selections *should not be fast, or rhythmically stimulating,* because such sounds incite the brain rather than soothe. Tempo (speed) consideration is important. Music for soothing the brain and body can never be too slow! Second, music needs to have limited auditory information—meaning large orchestral works produce too much auditory information that could agitate and confuse rather than soothe the brain, unless the orchestration is predominantly for strings and wind instruments, with minimal brass and percussion. Solo instrumental music, trios, quartets, and small chamber ensembles, solo piano, or piano with violin or cello, or just solo violin or cello, work very well (e.g., Bach Cello Suites or Violin Sonatas; Chopin piano music such as Nocturnes and Waltzes; Haydn, Handel, Mozart, Debussy, Ravel solo piano music, or calmer impressionistic orchestral music, etc.). The brain does not need an abundance of fast-paced auditory input. Parents must be quite selective about this. Major orchestral symphonies, such as those of Beethoven, Mahler, or Bruckner, are very complex in auditory information and will keep the brain "awake" attempting to process and perceive the information. Here we seek to *relieve* the brain of its cognitive duties rather than to activate them.

For newborns to toddlers, the best, and what I consider as ideal, music for pacification purposes is Native American natural Indian flute recordings! There are many that include only flute, without drumming, vocals, other instruments, or electronic sounds—just bare native, soothing flute! I recommend those most of all! At any point in a child's life, regardless of age, and often for caregivers as well, such music will serve to immediately reduce anxiety, and to calm the system. Much of Native American flute music is basically arrhythmic, in that the flow contains many pauses and silences, giving the brain and body a chance to relax, release tensions, and process acoustic information. Other music recordings tend not to provide enough mental space. Often, pure Native American flute music is played along with sounds of nature in the background—birds, wind, the sea, etc. This is extremely soothing and provides a sense of safety and security. Examples of recordings I have used in clinical work include *The Spirit Sings* (North Sound Series, Native American flute with nature) and Carlos Nakai's *Canyon Trilogy*. There are many others. I caution the provider to be certain that the music is pure flute, with no electronic tampering or additional instrumental accompaniments to detract from relaxation by providing additional acoustic information for the brain to process.

Feeding time

Pre-recorded music of happy, rhythmic tunes and songs, are recommended, some with lyrics that describe the task of sucking, or chewing, and that have *strong rhythmic pulse*, not fast, but *not too slow*, to be commensurate with chewing and sucking tempos of the child. If music is playing during feeding time, the brain will tend to focus on, and become rhythmically entrained (synchronized with the rhythm) to the music, and be less distracted.

Important: Here again, as with sleep time music, the recordings should be those in which music is played on acoustic instruments rather than electronically conjured, machine-made "fake" sounds. The tempo of the music should be not too slow, but not fast! The brain needs time to process acoustic information. Recorded music produced on acoustic instruments is difficult to find in this day and age of digitized life. But searching for acoustic instrumental music is worth the effort.

Music playtime with found objects

Music playtime is a very important part of creative and emotional development. Hundreds of books are available, through this publisher and many others, describing all kinds of musical games, puzzles, toys, and activities that can be undertaken among family members. Music stores and online sites for music education provide endless lists of music activity books and music-making materials. The caution here is *not to use toy instruments, but real ones*, no matter how small or large, because development of accurate pitch and discrimination in the auditory system is important, and toys are... toys! Toy items are not made to be authentic musical instruments that provide accurate sounds. If a child, like most children on the autism spectrum, has perfect pitch memory, then toys that present less than accurate pitches will impede future accurate pitch processing. If a child does not have perfect pitch memory, all the more reason to provide instruments with accurate tones to train the ear!

When using drums or tambourines, purchases should be from music stores that can supply good drum heads, even if plastic (though natural skin heads are preferred but are more vulnerable to destruction). Wind instruments such as recorders and kazoos should be real, not toys. Toy recorders that are purchased at party stores have terribly inaccurate pitches, and toy kazoos do not vibrate correctly! This is a no-no. In general, best to refrain from obtaining party-favor toy instruments. If a keyboard is used, this, too, should not be the tingling toy type, which is not scale-pitch accurate!

Music playtime is imperative for developing imagination, abstract and creative thinking, task organization, gross and fine motor skills, sense of self and other, for leadership and social skills training, sensory interaction practice, vocal and language progress, learning to "win" and "lose," and much more. Part of growing up involves activity schedules (rising, eating, bathing, schooling, etc.); music playtime must be part of the schedule! Every week, if not each day of the week, a time for music play can be designated and undertaken!

No need to have many musical instruments—in fact, the more a child uses "found objects" for making rhythm and music, the more the increase in imagination and creativity, and the more the expansion of auditory sound processing. Found objects include *any* mostly unbreakable item that can provide pitch or rhythm, from glasses filled with different levels of water, to cooking utensils, to floors, radiator and air conditioning grids, paper, chopsticks, scissors cutting in rhythm—virtually anything can become an instrument (also a flying object which, of course, requires careful parent supervision). I have conducted music groups with found objects that included such things as tin foil (crushing, tearing, rubbing against other items), note books and paper being torn or cut in rhythms, keys and cutlery clanging, brushes (great for sensory brushing in rhythm), hardware pieces and tubes that attach to rubber water hoses that we used as mouthpieces similar to those on French horns, alarm clocks, even cell phone tones—truly, *any* object or furniture, such as metal filing cabinets, can create rhythm and be organized into a musical work! (In fact, a classical music composer once composed an orchestral piece for garbage can lid solo that was actually performed in New York's Carnegie Hall!)

Learning to play an instrument

It's never too early to start music training!! By the time a child reaches age three, and absolutely by age six, consideration for musical and instrumental skills learning *should become part of the child's educational curriculum*. Many stringed instrument programs (e.g., Suzuki) begin at age three; as can piano. Ability depends on functionality of a child, and especially of any diagnosed or spectrum child. If an ASD diagnosis has been given, and spectrum level determined, *a child can begin an instrument with special adaptations for ability considerations*; which instrument would work best, which instructor, and music lessons vs. music therapy will be discussed in later chapters. However, the sooner a child begins to train on a musical instrument—even if just puttering on a drum, xylophone, or piano, or blowing a recorder (without structured lessons)—the better chance for advancing creativity, sensorimotor skills, attention, auditory and visual tracking, language attainment, and more.

Recommendation: While one is never too young or too old to begin learning music, *age three is absolutely the best time to begin*, and by age six at the latest, when possible! At this stage of development, the brain has already shed its excess neurons, etc., the cerebellum is ready to continue contributing adaptively to motor activities, and the frontal cortex (executive brain) is very ready to process cognitive information. Beginning instrumental training early can assure not only good brain and sensory development, but also the development of good upper body muscle tone, breath control, motor planning, auditory and visual processing, bilateral coordination, expressive language development, and many other characteristics that may later become obstacles to good development if not addressed early. Yes, it takes a bit of motivation and courage on the part of the caregiver, not to mention financing, but there are many programs available that present music skills learning, rhythmic pacing, and instrumental training.

Music and movement playtime

Once again, although I do not normally promote any particular form of training, here I do strongly want to recommend *Dalcroze Eurhythmics* music-movement classes and playtime, that can begin as young as three or four years of age. This unique, important, and fun experience, discussed in Chapter 4, provides rhythmic multisensory and motor stimulation that strengthen multitasking, sensory interactions, auditory development and attention, and motor planning, in a way that few other programs do. Any child, of any functional ability, will benefit from Dalcroze Eurhythmics classes. Dalcroze Eurhythmics and other rhythm and movement training classes can be found almost in every country.

Seven to 12 years: Music for social, physical, and sensory regulation

By this age, the child may have been diagnosed with some form of alternative function. If music has been incorporated into the life of the developing child since birth, the child reaching this age and possible diagnosis will be well able to continue interaction with music. By this age, music is usually part of the school curriculum. Here the parent of a spectrum or otherwise diagnosed child *must become a strong advocate for the child's inclusion in music classes.* For inclusion in a general music class (non-instrumental), the music instructor must be sensitized to the possibility of auditory constraints encumbering the child. This means concern for such things as classroom seating arrangements (which, by the way, also applies to any academic class), possibly discomforting instrumental timbres, breathing issues if the recorder is part of the general music class, inability to attend for the entire class, delays in information processing, and much more. These issues should not prevent the child from participating in the regular music class. Sensitivity training for the child's aide may be required, as well as for the instructor(s). Class participation may require frequent breaks. Consultation with a music therapist and allied therapists (occupational, speech, etc.) can help assuage some difficulties by eliciting suggestions for *adaptive interaction.* If child is in a school music class, shorter class time increments may be advisable. Ten minutes, break, ten more minutes, etc., allowing for positive redirection of anxieties, or for opportunities to leave the room for a few minutes to drink water and reorganize. Adaptations can include partnering with a "typically functioning" student; rotating seating arrangements depending on task; prompting or role-modeling by aide, instructor, or student partner; and shorter attendance segments (e.g., five minutes for recorder, ten minutes for singing, etc. at the discretion of the instructor and task requirement).

Bottom line: Inclusion in music class is a must. A well-trained aide or instructor will know how to redirect less preferred behaviors.

Instrumental skills acquisition in school

By third or fourth grade, school music programs usually begin to include instrumental lessons. This is an absolute must for any child, but especially a child with a spectrum or other diagnosis. *Parents must advocate for inclusion in instrumental learning.* No one can judge what abilities lie beneath the diagnosis! I cannot shout this out too loudly or often. I have provided music-based treatment services to spectrum, ADHD, and Down syndrome youngsters who ultimately displayed extensive talent and capacity for instrumental learning, while academic progress may have been limited. Five of the diagnosed youngsters I worked with in the past began to prefer that straight piano or stringed instrument lessons be included in the music-based treatment session! Two became such proficient pianists they won various music competition awards. Another is now a professional singer and actor! Two others studied stringed instruments, one on violin, and one on cello, that led to interest in the double bass. While none of these children could write an extended report or mathematical problem for school, or fully understand chemistry, biology, or physics, their genius lay in the abstract thinking of music. (In fact, some people think that perhaps Mozart's own behaviors may have been the result of Tourette's syndrome!)

Autism spectrum and other diagnosed children should definitely be included in instrumental skills learning classes. Yes, this may be a struggle to achieve, and learning the skills may be very slow, difficult, and seemingly unsuccessful. No matter. It must be undertaken, for a list of reasons that would result in another complete book! But in one sentence: *"Disability" does not mean "Inability"!* In fact, *"dis*ability" (the term) should be deleted from dictionaries. One is not disabled, but rather, *able* in an alternative way, other than in the expected "norm." Music class is about discovering *abilities*. From the ability to attend, experience abstract imagery (as in music notation = sound), to the mere discipline of being in a class of non-verbal expectations. What's more, instrumental skills training is said to advance mathematical skills (e.g., 2 quarter notes = 1 half note), vision and auditory tracking skills, depth perception, attention to detail, fine and gross motor skills, task endurance, and abstract thinking, in addition to all the sensory physiological and neurological coordinations. Best of all: playing an instrument in a group automatically develops socialization skills, one's sense of self and achievement, and a level of "able" functionality!

Music outside of school

Eurhythmics rhythm and movement classes (see Chapter 4), and instrumental training should continue, or begin, if this has not been undertaken sooner. Eurhythmics classes are group activities that can contribute to increasing social skills, in addition to sensorimotor regulation. Continuation of out-of-school instrumental lessons can also include group playing (e.g., Suzuki groups, band, string orchestras, choirs, etc., and many other options). The chapters herein titled "Music Lessons, Music Therapy, or Both?" (Chapter 4); "What Instrument Should I Choose for My Child?" (Chapter 5); "Lessons, Practice, and Penalties" (Chapter 6); and "Taking Your Child to a Concert" (Chapter 7) discuss various considerations regarding music interactions outside of school, that may be helpful in continuing music in the child's life.

Listening to music on CDs, especially music that involves the instrument(s) being studied, is a nice way to reinforce interest. The most productive activity is to *attend a live concert!* Observing music being played—the physicality, the emotional display, the manner of holding an instrument, the musician interactions, the drama, and more—absolutely reinforces productivity and motivation on the student learning an instrument. In addition, attending a live concert increases auditory sound location, discrimination, and visual/auditory interaction! This is not available when sitting alone in a room, plugged into earphones, just listening to a CD, because the mind/brain will wander away from the sound, and because this is an isolating activity. At a live concert, the brain will have difficulty wandering away due to the abundance of visual/ auditory stimulation happening everywhere, people coming and going, different attires, faces, scents, sizes, etc. (for a discussion on sensory-auditory overload at live concerts, see Chapter 7). Several youngsters I worked with loved attending rock concerts—and although the volume could be overwhelming, the light show and gyrations by the musicians on stage captivated such interest that the brain forgot about its auditory sensitivity! In addition, since rhythm stimulated the body to move, the movement also distracted from the auditory sensitivity. Several other children enjoyed opera or Broadway musicals, orchestral concerts, and children's concerts. Any live music concert is a valuable experience. Preference should be given to music the child prefers and likes, balanced as well with parental suggestions. There is no "bad" music—so a parent supports a child's interest by accepting the child's preferences. Parental suggestions can be positive as well. Attending a performance by Bon Jovi can be highly stimulating, while attending a piano recital can be "boring." Each is valid, and much depends on the relationship between parent and child, and the manner in which the child is prepared to attend a live performance of any kind, especially of classical music.

Music or sports
The continued interaction with music for this age group is important in setting the stage for "teen" year habits, tastes, social skills, and disciplined learning. Instrumental skills training, regardless of level of progress, should continue. Disciplined learning and emotional regulation comes with the territory. By this age, though, some sports activities begin to enter the curriculum. That's good...but... *music should not be replaced by a sport.* In fact, the more these two activities interact, the better the furtherance of proprioception, vestibular, and motor-planning function due to the auditory/visual and rhythmic movement training gained through instrumental learning! Indeed physical development is important, but aesthetics and non-verbal emotional communication should not be replaced by sports.

Both music and sports have a place in one's day or week, and the either/or approach would be an unfortunate decision. A youngster can undertake both—sports and music both involve rhythmic motor planning. Eurhythmics and music skills train for such rhythmic integration! Auditory/visual interaction is crucial in depth perception and sports, and vital in music! Do both, and see how well your child responds! Music for cognition, sensory concerns, task discipline, mathematical and spatial skills, motor control, socialization, and anxiety-reducing emotional expression; sports for motor planning, upper/lower body coordination, strategic thinking, socialization skills, muscle tone, vestibular and proprioceptive advancement—both music and sports interact for the betterment of the ASD, ADHD, or other diagnosed child. No. Not either/or. *Both*.

Ten years and up: Music for the cultured adult "teen"

Functional age and chronological age are not necessarily at the same level. No matter. By the time your child reaches the chronological age of ten years and up, your child will (we hope) have had at least five or six years of interaction with music and movement, in some way or other. At this stage of development, the higher-functioning ASD or otherwise diagnosed young person is indicating more fully his/her personality traits, interests, needs, desires, abilities, and behavioral characteristics. Regardless of level of cognition or language ability, the person *inside* the diagnosis is coming forward. This age is also the time of conflicts, hormonally, parentally, socially, and most of all, *conflict with "self."* A higher-functioning diagnosed child will, by now, understand his/her alternative function abilities, or a sense of "being different." The psycho-emotional piece looms. Now music's role is even more significant. Self-expression through playing an instrument, especially for the youngster with limited language abilities, the sharing of a creative activity with another, being part of a creative group, letting rhythm continue to train the system into an organized response, and much more, become important in the developing soon-to-be adult!

The athletic child may now want to quit music and continue with sports. This can often produce conflicts. If both music and sports were included in the youngster's curriculum, I argue that parents should *continue music alongside sports* activities. While sports is age-dependent, music is lifelong. And the discipline of music training will continue to enhance sensorimotor, cognitive, and emotional function.

At this age, also, group music is highly recommended! Anyone can clang a triangle or cymbal (with proper prompt from an aide); anyone can hum into a kazoo to sing along (even in a band or orchestra!). There are very few activities that enhance socialization skills as delightfully as the participation in an orchestra or band. And by age 13, middle school, and high school years, this activity is all the more important! *No, this is not the time to eliminate music from one's development into adulthood.*

One last note: Attending *live performances* is recommended all the more for this age group, especially to continue the adaptive processes of auditory/visual adaptation and *social coping*. Any music, from Bach to rock, works wonders in live performances.

Conclusion

In sum, our chapter culminates with the hope that readers will keep the above suggestions in mind, because emotion and emotional expression contribute to a *positive quality of life* for any human being, and especially for children on the autism spectrum and those with other diagnoses, in addition to encouraging learning and social participation. Feeling good about oneself, and the world around us, is important for growth; and music, which requires no language to express feelings and needs, assists in many ways the attainment of good feelings. A child managing a variety of diagnosis-related symptoms, of any kind, undergoes a great deal of emotional anxiety, sadness, and especially isolation. Sensory-wise, the planet is a difficult environment! Crowds and society make unreasonable demands for "normalcy"—whatever that means. Most of all, a child with limited expressive language, who has no other way of expressing interests and needs other than by "acting out" can use music to creatively "act out," expressing him/herself without the need for words! From infancy to adulthood and beyond, music reaches deep inside of emotional brain structures (amygdala et al.), to calm, soothe, release anxieties, and regulate sensorimotor and psycho-emotional responses.

Music, and music training, no matter how slow the learning process might be, are worth the efforts. This is the *emotional sense-ability* of the musical brain. Believe in its power!

PROVIDING MUSIC IN A CHILD'S LIFE

———

CHAPTER 4

MUSIC LESSONS, MUSIC THERAPY, OR BOTH?

It's easy to play any musical instrument: all you have to do is touch the right key at the right time and the instrument will play itself.

JOHANN SEBASTIAN BACH

When and how can a parent choose whether music lessons, music therapy, or both should be sought for the student? Such decisions probably will be based on the developmental agenda, the youngster's age, ability and interests, financial considerations, and commitment to choice. Once a determination is made, the ability of a diagnosed child to acquire skills comes into play in undertaking the next step, and knowledge of the differences between "lessons" and "therapy" will determine which direction is best. This brief chapter provides some considerations and recommendations for attaining adequate musical skills training and/or appropriate music-based treatment.

Music lessons

Your child loves music. A diagnosed health condition does not detract from that love. Each time your child passes a piano, s/he touches it with glee. Each time the child passes a drum, you hear rhythms. Whenever the radio or TV includes music, especially featuring a particular tune, instrument or voice, the child's attention is drawn to the sounds. These observations signal that it is time to seek formal music lessons, as I have been advocating throughout this book. In Chapter 5 ("What Instrument Should I Choose for My Child?") I share that research has been supporting the opinion that learning to play an instrument develops the brain and sensory systems in many positive ways. I also suggest that by the time a child turns three or four years of age, while singing, blowing into a recorder, and humming into a kazoo is great fun, the piano is the best instrument on which to begin training, for many reasons (see "The piano" section in Chapter 5). Consideration can also include training on a stringed, brass, wind, or rhythm instrument, depending on the child's age, interest(s), auditory acuity, and developmental functional age/stage.

So, what do music lessons involve? At a glance it means that someone who is proficient on an instrument will impart training to a child, through various means, materials, and meetings. Music training means learning music notation, that is, learning to read music in order to deliver the prescribed sounds; it also means understanding rhythmic notation, and embodying a sense of pulse in order to organize accurate delivery of notated music; and, above all, it means learning how to interpret the notation and the composer's emotional intent, and express the feelings of both the composer and the performer of the piece. Therefore, it can be thought that learning to play an instrument, and learning to read and interpret musical notation, can ultimately result in emotional and mental organization and self-awareness, and empathetic understanding of the deeper experience of another human being through his/her composition. This type of logic and awareness is derived cumulatively, and somewhat indirectly, through the instructor's ability to impart the essence of music through teaching an instrument and the understanding of notation details (e.g., soft, loud, crescendo, etc.).

Music lessons are most often undertaken one-on-one, at the instructor's studio, although some teachers do travel to private homes to teach. My preference is for the student *to go to the instructor's studio*, to the "classroom," because attending a lesson at a designated setting (as such) often results in the training being accepted as a serious, "official" learning endeavor. In-home lessons are often less "private" and could include habitual in-home behaviors, routines, scattered toys, siblings running around, and various interruptions. In essence, a "home environment" is not always conducive to becoming a specialty "learning environment." Any other type of extra-curricular training, such as sports, art classes, drama, dance, takes place *outside* the home. Music lessons are equally best undertaken within a music environment, outside the home. This often means complex scheduling, especially if siblings have their various extra-curricular activities. However, I urge parents to think of music lessons as equal to any other extra-curricular tasks, and to schedule lessons at a teacher's studio, in the best interest of learning. A sacrifice? Yes. Is it the best approach? Yes. Furthermore, in addition to instrument training at the teacher's studio, I recommend investigating the possibility of obtaining rhythmic movement interaction—particularly classes in Dalcroze

Eurhythmics. This is especially recommended for children on the autism spectrum, and with other diagnoses (ADHD, Down syndrome, language and cognitive delays, etc.).

A word about Dalcroze Eurhythmics

Rhythm is the first fundamental element of music! Without good rhythmic performance that organizes a piece of music, the intent of the composition is convoluted. Rhythm training, actually learning to embody the mathematical structure that holds a piece of music together, is inherent in all music lessons. And, the best way to engender precise rhythmic expression is through additional classes in eurhythmics movement. Through this very special training activity, music students gain not only rhythmic acuity, but also insight into musical expression: *phrasing, dynamics, form* and *structure* within a piece of music. Briefly described, the term *eurhythmics* came into being in early 20th-century English, to define "good rhythm": *eu* meaning "well" + *rhythm* + *ics*. The word came into being as a result of the music training philosophy and approach of the Swiss music instructor, Émile Jaques-Dalcroze (1865–1950).

Jaques-Dalcroze carried out music education and rhythmic training by incorporating body movements to reflect, synchronize with, and internalize (embody, entrain with) music fundamentals, beginning with *rhythm*, and including *melody* (tonality), *timbre* (sound texture), *dynamics* (volume), *harmony*, and *form* (phrase, structure, continuity, etc.)—the six basic elements of music. Jaques-Dalcroze opined that music students were deficient in delivering appropriate rhythmic accuracy and interpretive understanding of the pieces they were playing. He observed that the training of musicians was greatly lacking in the teaching of music's profound fundamentals and delivery system thereof, especially of rhythm, but also phrase, dynamics, and the emotional sagacity of various harmonies and form structures. His philosophy introduced the idea that there was a distinct relationship between rhythm and body movement. He also believed that movement blockages within various areas of the body were indicators of physical rhythmic blockages—that the body was not free to move rhythmically and efficiently due to muscular tensions. He was of the opinion that relaxation was the ultimate requirement in support of the body and movement, and that *breathing*, the fundamental rhythmic body activity (in addition to the heart), was essential for obtaining relaxation! These views resulted from his studies of human function, whereby, through some experimentation, he began to realize that the source of all rhythm, including music, is found *within* the body—heartbeats, breathing, circadian rhythms such as sleep/wake/hormonal cycles, walking, running, swaying, bouncing, etc. He surmised that the body, itself, is the best vehicle for instilling rhythmic sensibility since the energies of many body rhythms are simulated within the energies of music rhythm, and because *playing or singing music involves rhythmic physical movement and breathing*.

Jaques-Dalcroze also ascertained that the full understanding and incorporation of the essence of music's various essentials in playing a piece must first be sensed and experienced in physical movement. Thus, he was convinced that the most effective way to achieve this is through the *embodiment* (internalization) of rhythmic relationships through kinesthetic activities reflecting the language of music, in order for these to become *intuitive—instinctive*! He believed that such embodiment, produced and perpetuated through movement and breathing exercises, will not only be effective in expressing the music correctly through instinctive, internalized awareness and response, but will also derive bodily self-awareness, intuition, and naturally spontaneous reactions when performing the music's intended expression. In essence, eurhythmics is the coordination of ultimate *entrainment (synchronizing) with* and *embodiment (internalizing) of* music rudiments, attaining the highest perception of self and music for achieving the peak level of musical expression. Ultimately, Jaques-Dalcroze ascertained that, since music moves in time and space, this kinesthetic component to music education presents the definitive unification of *mind and body*—the integration of the physical with the emotional sensitivity required in the aesthetic expression of music. In short, the training of musicians must be *holistic*!

Eurhythmics movement training is extremely helpful to children on the autism spectrum! Movement, sensory deficiencies, body organization, and auditory processing issues are worrisome factors in ASD behaviors, and many result from inaccurate motor planning and auditory/sensory misperception. Eurhythmics movement classes directly address and help to regulate movement, sensory perception, and especially *ear training*. To respond with movement, the student must react to an auditory (musical) cue. S/he must carefully listen to the music in order to adequately reflect its content through movement. Eurhythmics insists on vocalization, and improvisation on an instrument—a unique musical thought process. And much more. Eurhythmics in and of itself can serve as a therapeutic intervention, without being designated as such. Amazing results are obtained, physiologically, emotionally, and musically, when a child on the spectrum becomes involved with eurhythmics movement activities. In addition to my use of eurhythmics movement in my own music-based clinical work with children on the spectrum and other diagnoses, I have included eurhythmics activities during every one of my piano teaching sessions with diagnosed as well as "typically functioning" students. Many instrumental instructors have some training in Dalcroze Eurhythmics and can incorporate such movement activities within the lesson. If not, readers might investigate online where eurhythmics classes are available within their community or region. An internet search for Dalcroze Eurhythmics national and international organizations will provide pertinent information. Some Dalcroze locations are listed in Chapter 9.

Be aware that Dalcroze Eurhythmics is a very distinct rhythm/ movement approach to music training, above and beyond just studying an instrument. I speak here of not just any ordinary "music and rhythm" music class. Dalcroze Eurhythmics instructors have undergone several years of classwork, and many accrue various certifications in this training after years of study at distinguished Dalcroze schools. In my undergraduate music training at Carnegie Mellon University, it was required that students participate in two years of Dalcroze training, in addition to the various music theory, history, and instrumental classes. I can personally attest to the importance of this activity in my own performances, my teaching skills, and especially my music-based clinical work. Readers can find more about this in my recent book *Eurhythmics for Autism and Other Neurophysiologic Diagnoses: A Sensorimotor Music-Based Treatment Approach* (2015, Jessica Kingsley Publishers).

How to find and select a music teacher

Finding a music teacher who understands the needs and habits of a child on the spectrum, or with any other diagnosis (Down syndrome, ADHD, etc.) is not a simple endeavor. Musical expertise of the instructor is, of course, important. But more important is whether the instructor: (a) has ever worked with a diagnosed or ASD child; (b) understands some of the symptomatic behaviors that could intrude in a lesson; (c) has expectations that may be unequal to the abilities of the student; (d) would enjoy the challenges of teaching a child of different abilities; (e) will understand deficits and learning styles of the student (this is needed for teaching *any* child, diagnosed or typical). The challenges are many, but the astute parent or caregiver will thoroughly interview an instructor, asking questions that will reveal whether a teacher is a "match" to the child's interests, abilities, needs, and personality.

Given the questions that the parent will be asking when interviewing the instructor, the best place to begin the search for an instructor is through the child's school music teachers. If the child is in pre-school (age three to four years), there are usually in-house teachers, or adjunct persons who conduct music classes with the children. Such persons may be music teachers in private, or may have a network of persons interested in working with special needs children, to teach piano or violin (at this young age). In addition, the child's behaviors in school music gatherings will advise the parent as to the best type of instruction and instructor to seek. In addition to school music teachers, there are in many locations music training organizations of various levels—local university music departments, private music schools, conservatories, music stores that include instrumental training, and various special needs support groups that can share information about instructors and organizations.

Caution: Start at the top. Seek university or conservatory recommendations that can more or less guarantee good training. Not just any teacher will do! In addition to background training excellence, the personality characteristics of the instructor are vital to the development of a positive and successful student/teacher relationship. Too strict or too lenient approaches often do not achieve good training. The parent/caregiver will "interview" the instructor by posing some of the following questions, in addition to investigating music educator background qualifications (where s/he was trained, etc.):

- How do you feel about teaching a child of different abilities?
- What are your particular approaches and expectations as a teacher?
- Would you consider yourself to be strict, flexible, patient?
- What are your achievement expectations for the student? Practice habits?
- Do you have experience working with a special-needs student? Please explain.
- Can you give me an overview of your strengths as a music teacher?
- Are you trained in Dalcroze Eurhythmics, and do you apply that in teaching?
- What do you expect of the parent?
- Can you provide one or two references of parents with whom I can chat?

Although these few questions seem benign, many instructors may resist responding—which, of course, will immediately provide some insight into the personality and attitude of the teacher. Attaining a comprehensive overview of the instructor, as a person, musician, and teacher is important, because the special-needs diagnosed student needs someone who is patient, kind, congenial, and committed to helping the student learn, regardless of "abilities," and whose expectations are flexible and *adaptive* to the level and sequence of learning required by the special student! You will need to know whether the teacher can accept slow achievement; whether instruction can be parceled in smaller increments; whether adaptive notation and hand positions can be interwoven with standard approaches and expectations. In essence, you want the teacher to *inspire* and *motivate* students to try their best, *without parental interference*, as suggested in Chapter 6 discussing practice routines. This, of course, applies to any and all types of students, typical or diagnosed. Anyone seeking instrumental instructions must feel "safe" in the hands of the instructor, especially since music involves emotions!

Certain instruction requires parental participation—particularly Suzuki violin and piano training. Be aware, however, that most such training centers do not often have the background or experience in teaching special-needs children, are rather inflexible in their expectations and training approaches, and may not be the best alternative to music instruction for a special-needs student, because of the stricter achievement expectations. As stated several times throughout this book, "achievement" is not necessarily the goal of a special-needs students studying an instrument. Focus, coordination of body and brain, cognition, sensory integrative development, socialization, pure enjoyment, and quality of life predominate as objectives for instrumental training, actually for any child, but especially for one who is diagnosed. If the teacher you interview does not agree with these objectives, move on and find another instructor. Once a selection is made, your commitment to continual weekly lessons is required, even if/when "music homework" (practice) is lax. This is discussed further in Chapter 6 ("Lessons, Practice, and Penalties").

Would music *therapy* be a better way to begin?

The term *music therapy* is often erroneously applied to any type of music activity that seems to pacify, relax, or entertain a person. That is incorrect! There is a difference between music as *therapeutic succor* that entertains recreationally, and music as a *therapy treatment*. Music therapy is, in fact, a *treatment* with goals and objectives applying music elements to address particular physiological, cognitive, sensorimotor, and/or psycho-emotional functional problems. It involves the use of any or all of the six basic elements of music—rhythm, melody (pitch), timbre, dynamics, harmony, form—in *clinical* ways that intervene to treat various diagnoses, conditions, syndromes, or needs. In various circumstances, music therapy may be covered by medical insurers, but that varies from place to place. There are many books and papers outlining the work of music therapy, including various ones I have written, so I will not endeavor to define the work in this brief chapter, but rather, I will leave the search for further information to readers (searches on Google, Amazon, and music therapy organizations can provide resources for further investigation). Here we will discuss why, when, and how to find a music-based clinician, and whether therapy or lessons would be the best way to begin music skills training of a diagnosed child.

For children diagnosed on the autism spectrum, the level of functional ability will determine whether *treatment* with music would be preferable to direct music *training*. Or, would an integrated use of both approaches work best, providing "treatment" through instruction? Here, again, the parent can seek advice from school (academic and music) teachers and various allied practitioners (occupational therapists, speech therapists, etc.) to confirm the level of functional abilities of the child. If the child can attend to information (focus), if the child indicates the ability to replicate an action, if the child can retain and recall cognitive information, if the child can stick to a task for any length of time beyond a fleeting moment, and if the child's interest in an activity, subject, or skill is continuous, then straight lessons can be undertaken. However, if any of these "ifs" is negative, or if there are sensorimotor, auditory, or cognitive issues inhibiting learning somehow, perhaps it would be best to begin first with *music-based treatment* (i.e., music therapy), especially if eurhythmics can be applied, that can correct some of the deficits adequately to prepare the child for learning to play an instrument. Beginning music lessons with music therapy can gradually add a level of instrumental skills training along with eurhythmics movement and music concepts, as a portion of the treatment, thus "killing two birds with one stone," so to speak.

Many professional, experienced music therapists treat sensorimotor, cognitive, and other deficits as part of music sessions, while also teaching piano, violin, or other instrumental skills, as a portion of the treatment, since instrumental training can be as much "treatment" as straight therapy interventions. For special-needs students who are on the less-functional level of the spectrum, I recommend only music therapy first, to address, alter, and improve various deficits that could impede music learning. After many months, and sometimes many years, of music-based treatment, developmental progress will indicate whether or not there is an opportunity to begin including some instrumental (or vocal) training as part of the treatment plan. I have had the experience of providing straight music-based treatment interventions (music therapy) for several years to youngsters on the spectrum, or with Down syndrome or ADHD, that eventually led to piano lessons becoming part of the treatment session. This led to the elimination of the "treatment" portion altogether, to become straight piano lessons, with amazing cognitive and skills results! Several of the clients had become proficient enough to perform and win competitions, to teach piano to diagnosed students, and to gain employment playing piano for pre-school music classes! The possibilities are unlimited, but the determination will be made by the parents, school teachers, and the music-based clinician.

For the parent, the choice is whether to seek "treatment" with music, or direct music skills training. Since school inclusion of special-needs youngsters into music classes and instrumental training becomes available by grades 3 and 4, a student's interests and strengths can be determined from such participation. *I advocate continual skills instruction within, and outside of school, to reinforce skills development.* Also, include eurhythmics! Furthermore, since piano skills are not taught in school, and since I suggest beginning with piano training regardless of interest in other instruments, school music training can be supplemented with external studies— the more, the better!

Finding a music therapist

Music therapy is a specifically *credentialed* profession! Credentials include, in addition to various degree levels in music therapy, a Board Certification, and in some geographic areas may also include local licensure, depending on the country or location (Canada, different US States, European countries, etc.) in which music therapists practice. In the United States, for instance, the gold standard of credentials is the MT-BC, Music Therapist–Board Certified. Certification is provided by the Certification Board For Music Therapists, a national organization monitoring the professionalism and ethics of the music-based clinician. The MT-BC credential indicates an accomplished undertaking of specified courses and internships, degrees up to doctorate, and knowledge to successfully complete a five-hour qualifying examination. In addition, it is required that every five years, the credential be renewed based on having undertaken a minimum of 100 continuing education credits, accrued through courses, publications, presentations, supervisory activities, ethics training, conference attendance, and more. Countries across the globe have their own specific credentialing processes. Parents seeking music-based clinicians must be certain that such credentials are part of the clinician's achievements, or they should not be hired under the guise of "professional music therapists." Here, again, many musicians who volunteer in hospitals and elsewhere often refer to themselves as "music therapists"—but this is erroneous, and parents need to be aware. It is easy for parents and others to be confused, so I suggest careful investigation of credentials and consultation with music therapy associations that exist in most countries around the world, prior to scheduling an appointment.

How to find a credentialed clinician? Most countries have music therapy organizations that house lists of their country's credentialed clinicians. In the United States, the American Music Therapy Association (AMTA) and the Certification Board for Music Therapists have lists of practitioners in regions throughout the country, that parents can obtain. In the UK there is the British Association for

Music Therapy; in Canada, the Canadian Association for Music Therapy; and so on (see listing in Chapter 9). If a parent is unsure of how to find an association, a search for universities that provide music therapy training can also yield lists of associations that represent the profession in their region or country. A list of therapist names does not suggest "recommended clinicians," but is just a listing of clinicians in an area. Parents and others will determine whom to contact based on geographic location, itemized expertise, and perhaps referrals by others. There is also the World Federation of Music Therapy, which can provide information on music therapy practices in a particular area of the world (see Chapter 9).

How to interview a music therapist

Understanding the difference between a music *teacher* and a music *therapist* will guide parents and others toward determining what would be in the best interest of the child's music skills training, or treatment of the diagnosis. Once the determination is made to begin training with music-based treatment, and the search for a credentialed, professional clinician has begun, an interview (or several) will best influence the selection.

To begin with, many of the same requirements and questions that apply to a music teacher are included in deciding the most appropriate music-based clinician. This includes (a) the experience the clinician has with a child diagnosed similarly to your child—ASD, Down, Angelman, ADHD, developmental and language delays, etc.; (b) professional credentials; and, most important, (c) specific clinical treatment approach; (d) references for speaking with other parents or clients; and more. Here are a dozen interview questions to ask, that will reveal clinician's attitudes, demeanor, and clinical approach(es):

- Please tell me about your experience in working with this population.

- What is your clinical approach, and how do you assess priority of clinical needs?

- How do you develop goals and objectives, and how do you track progress?

- What is your approach to handling behavioral outbursts or other events?

- Are you familiar with sensorimotor and "fear" behaviors, and how do you treat those?

- Some clinicians are more comfortable addressing the immediate "behavior," or cognitive or language problems, while others want to focus on deeper, sensorimotor physiological issues. Which are you?

- Do you tend to lead the session, or do you follow the child's lead?

- What are your strengths as a music-based clinician?

- How do you feel about yourself—as a person, as a musician, as a clinician?

- Do you play or teach instrumental skills? Piano? Other? Would you include that in treatment? Are you trained in eurhythmics and do/would you apply it?

- Have you published? Do you have any of your written material that I can read, and do you communicate openly with the parent about the child's needs and progress?

- Would you provide some client names with whom I can speak?

A parent seeking music-based treatment for his/her child prior to engaging an instrument teacher *must feel very comfortable and secure that the clinician is not a "beginner,"* has plenty of experience with the population, with accrued positive progress, knows what s/he is and will be doing in approaching treatment of various physiological, sensorimotor, emotional, cognitive deficits, and will go beyond just playing musical games and providing musical "baby-sitting" services in a session. Music therapy is not a recreational activity, it is *clinical.* Music therapy is a serious profession, even if playing music is fun! It is a *treatment*, as already stated, and clinicians must be well-credentialed experts who understand a diagnosis, and the function of the human body and brain, and must have an astute "clinical eye" to provide treatment appropriate to the diagnosis and needs. The seeker of music therapy for the child must, therefore, feel comfortable interviewing and gaining insight into the expectations and expertise of the clinician. Music therapy services can be more costly than pure music lessons, therefore a parent will want to know as much as possible about who s/he is employing and providing the best treatment for the child.

Summary review

Learning to play an instrument—or, taking lessons on an instrument, even if "learning" is incidental—has enormous power to develop good brain function, visual-auditory tracking skills, fine-motor coordination, attention and focus, and a sense of achievement (however minimal it might be), and to provide an opportunity for musical social interaction. Any child, and especially a child with a diagnosis, is capable of undertaking some instrumental music skills learning. I firmly advocate the study of an instrument—at any level or ability to achieve even minimal success. I urge readers to investigate the extensive research verifying and praising the value of music lessons in child development. (Readers can search the internet asking for research in "music training and the brain", "instrumental music training and child development", and similar search titles that will yield many research papers.) Also strongly recommended is music training with additional Dalcroze Eurhythmics movement interactions, as part of instrumental training and/or as music therapy interventions.

In reviewing how to select a teacher or a music-based clinician, it is clear that a strong "interview" process will provide the seeker with the best information and advice for determining whether music lessons or music therapy would be the best way to begin, and which instructor or clinician will be advisable. The parent or seeker of services should not be shy about asking pertinent questions, and determining the best option, based on the advice of school personnel, various associations (for therapy), and schools of music (conservatories, academies, universities, etc.), and on personal interviews with teachers and clinical providers. Most important—music encounters and training will provide excellent development and behavioral function for *any* child, and especially for the child of special needs on the autism spectrum.

An informed parent or caregiver will be attracted to an informed and well-trained music teacher and/or clinician. It will take patience and time, but is worth the effort.

CHAPTER 5

WHAT INSTRUMENT SHOULD I CHOOSE FOR MY CHILD?

Setting my mind on a musical instrument was like falling in love.
All the world seemed bright and changed.

WILLIAM CHRISTOPHER HANDY, MUSICIAN (1873–1958)

A word about studying a musical instrument

Over the past several decades there has been extensive research on the role and impact of music, and music training, on the brain and body. Many researchers throughout the world have compiled data to indicate that, indeed, the learning of a musical instrument influences the development of more efficient brains, and brain-body functions. An example of such findings is an article in *The Strad* magazine that summarized research conducted by psychiatrists in Vermont, USA, who discovered that instrumental training can have an important impact on the many physiological, sensory, psycho-emotional, and cognitive difficulties that affect the diagnosed populations.[5] The article brings out that researchers found instrumental playing to have had an impact upon motor and behavior-regulating areas of the brain! Instrumental practice was found also to influence cortical thickness related to executive functioning, including working memory, attention control, as well as organization and planning ahead. Further it was stated that in children with musical backgrounds the brain was impacted in areas that play critical roles in *inhibitory control*, as well as aspects of emotion processing.

These findings are not surprising, since the interest, motivation and discipline required in learning a musical instrument increases the brain's ability to become attentive, focused, detail-oriented, and to call for organized, multitasking abilities of the body. This implicates multiple motor-planning and muscular organization skills. Here are a few reasons for undertaking instrumental learning:

- cognition and mental focus

- task attention and stick-to-it-iveness

- auditory and visual coordination, tracking, sequencing

- eye-hand coordination

---

5   *The Strad*, January 5, 2015: www.thestrad.com/cpt-latests/study-finds-musical-training-may-focus-attention-reduce-anxiety-children

- extended visual, auditory, mental attention

- sequential memory and recall

- bilateral arm, hand, and fine motor coordination

- abstract information processing and creative thinking

- anticipation and planning ahead

- rhythm embodiment (entrainment) yielding systemic organization

- self-discipline and self-awareness

- accomplishment and self-esteem

- socialization skills in group music making.

These are just a few areas of function impacted by learning a musical instrument. Yes, you say, many other activities could yield some of the same benefits. Okay—but few other activities address the sensory and emotional systems, *whole* brain/*whole* body, along with auditory/visual/physiological organization, while also providing the *creative motivation* that music provides. Playing an instrument is not a sport—it is an *aesthetic, emotional experience* yielding self-expression and emotional expression that few other experiences can yield. Why not plan it as part of the child's developmental curriculum?

Where and how to begin— recorder, kazoo, the voice!

The voice is the first, most natural instrument given to human beings. Vocalizations communicate needs, desires, opinions, whether these are articulated in the form of spoken language or just inflective sounds. In contrast to other animals, the human being has only a limited number of communicative vocal "calls," such as screaming, laughing, crying, moaning when in pain, sighing. In children on the spectrum, or with various other diagnoses, vocal calls are often limited to crying, screaming, or shouting. As we know, vocalization skills are important for spoken language. Inflective toning of words communicates feelings. This often needs to be taught, and learned by a developmentally delayed youngster. The child will hear "singing" everywhere, from mother's lullaby, to recorded children's songs, to religious observances. But singing, as a music activity, is less frequently undertaken by many children on the spectrum. This musical activity needs much more encouragement.

To capitalize on this in order to help develop positive non-verbal vocal communication, and to enhance breath control, inner sensory vibrations, and more, I recommend *hum–hum–hum* (kazoo), *blow–blow–blow* (recorder), *sing–sing–sing* (voice)! (None of these actions requires particular training, although if interest and inclination looms, formal recorder or vocal instructions can be pursued.) Encourage the child to copy sounds, to make unusual sounds, to sing songs. The kazoo is a wonderful way to encourage use of voice, because in order to obtain a sound from a kazoo, one must put this little instrument between one's lips, and hum into it. Vibrations provide excellent oral motor stimulation, and use of one's own voice, even when spoken language is unavailable to the child. The recorder enhances a breath-controlled inhale–exhale process that provides tones. When possible, the pressing down of fingers to cover the holes on the recorder can yield a tune, and also serves as an excellent fine-motor activity. And since the recorder is held with both hands, at front center of the body, the child's brain immediately receives midline information! (Accurate information about where is the body's "midline" helps the brain determine the body's "map" and position in relation to its interaction with the environment and eternal space—what and where is *center, left, right, up, distance determinations,* etc.) Eyes, tongue, hands all face front at midline. Everyone in the family can join in to play recorder, or hum into a kazoo, and sing together, providing a group interaction for everyone.

As youngsters reach school age, some involvement in recorder playing, and in group singing can follow. Singing in a chorus is a group activity. Any choir, religious, dramatic, or school choir, will go far in developing not only use of voice and breath control, some social skills, and interpersonal relationships. The kazoo, and singing, brings eyes forward, encourages visual center focus, and the following of non-verbal directives provided by the music (when to sing loud, soft, etc.). Singing should be part of the child's musical life and encouraged on a continual basis, even if other instrumental training is taking place.

Caution: A spectrum child with perfect pitch (an excellent ear, detecting in-or-out-of-tune pitches) may not wish to sing in a group that may have singers who are "out-of-tune." Also, excessive timbre (sound-quality) information emitted by a choir group may appear problematic to the child's auditory system. Singing alone should still be encouraged, whenever possible. Group singing is important, but does need to be considered in relation to the child's auditory processing. By the way, this problem is not limited to diagnosed children. Many "typically functioning" children, especially those who might have perfect pitch, can have discomforts when participating in choirs. This is a consideration for any child.

The piano

The sooner that *instrumental* training can begin, the better (even while singing is going on!). From the age of three and up, certain instruments provide the best opportunity for musical as well as physiological training. The question about which instrument to select for a young child can be answered in several ways. First, what are the musical interests of the child? Is the child drawn to a certain sound quality, or a particular instrument? Preference can go far to maintain a child's continuing interest in the particular instrument. This, of course, goes without saying. However, my suggestion is to begin instrumental lessons on the piano. There may be resistance, difficulty sitting for an extended amount of time, and other issues. You may be shouting about your own interests, for instance, *I hated the piano! Mother forced me do it!* Okay. The piano does not have to be loved, or even enjoyed, but for developmental purposes, both physical and mental, learning to play this particular instrument will yield a multitude of positive physiological and cognitive results, over the long run.

As I state in my book *Music Therapy, Sensory Integration and the Autistic Child* (2002, Jessica Kingsley Publishers), keyboard instruction and training is especially invaluable in developing many areas of sensory and physiological function, beginning with *eye-hand coordination*—required in writing skills! In addition, since both right and left arms, hands, and fingers participate, often in parallel motion, simultaneously, in the same or contrary manners when playing a keyboard instrument, many bilateral upper body physiological issues are immediately addressed, from the motor-planning and muscle-tone to mind–body coordination. Furthermore, both hands use fine-motor actions in similar ways, so that left and right sides of the brain can reinforce each other's motor-planning.

Several of my autism spectrum diagnosed young clients began studying piano with me as part of their therapy session, and amazing results occurred in their abilities to organize limb motor-plans, cognition, memory, visual sequential tracking, and attention to details. Reading music notation is, after all, an abstract "picture of tones"—it's a dot on a line or space, indicating a particular location on an instrument that ultimately yields a designated pitch. To learn to read music notation is akin to learning to read a foreign language—but there is no need cognitively to comprehend a linguistic message. In short, when a youngster is able to undertake actual deciphering of dots on a page in order to render a "tune," this is the most advanced cognitive activity that will ever be required of the brain! And this yields the ability to generalize information, something that is often extremely difficult for a child on the spectrum.

Furthermore, in piano training, the reading of two different clefs, the symbols on each indicating two different things—one clef indicating information for the left hand, the other indicating tones to be played by the right hand—is a highly complex comprehension function! Yet this has been achieved by most of the youngsters with whom I have worked. What's more, this achievement had great impact upon the students' school reading skills! Navigating the reading of two different clefs can be a bit challenging. One young student would play one hand at a time first, playing with the right hand while pointing to the notation line with his left hand, and vice versa. This secured excellent visual attention and tracking ability. Then, after several such repetitions, the student played both hands together, and had to follow the notation sequence visually, independently, taking in both treble and bass clefs simultaneously, the brain developing its strategies of eye movements (sort of zig-zagging up and down between clefs), since I would not be pointing to the notation. This ultimately increased the student's visual tracking and spatial comprehension abilities.

There are situations in which learning to read music may be difficult or unattainable. There are methods, such as Suzuki piano training that uses the rote method of learning, similar to that used in Suzuki violin training (see below). This involves memory and imitation of music patterns, rather than the actual reading of music notation. This approach, or a combination of reading and rote learning, can still bring about excellent training and focus. One method does not detract from another. In any manner, learning to play the piano is a complete multitasking opportunity to coordinate mind–body regulation. It enables the visual, auditory, tactile, and motor sensory systems to operate simultaneously. Parents of many children I have worked with indicated that since the inclusion of piano training, visual attention to details, and upper-body motor planning and muscle tone have increased. Since the piano is an instrument within the percussion group, arm muscles and joints are continuously providing energy exertion through pressing down the keys, along with proprioception information to the brain, eventually strengthening muscle tone and writing skills.

So, whether providing just piano lessons, or piano lessons as part of music therapy, the undertaking of learning to play the piano is the best place to begin, especially with young children on the spectrum. The sooner, the better. Meanwhile, the parent must set aside aspirations of success and stardom, or wondrous achievements, or concert heights. If that talent looms, great. But that should *not* be the purpose of engaging in piano skills training, at least not at the start. Below are some more reasons to provide piano lessons, and the less you, the parent, expect to raise another Vladimir Horowitz or Arthur Rubinstein, the more successful the child will be. It is enough to enjoy the fact that the student must learn to read two parallel but different clefs on which the notation is placed for right or left hand! (Most other instruments require the reading of only one clef.)

In addition to the major cognitive and motor-planning bilateral skills required in piano playing, starting instrumental training with piano lessons also develops the musical ear since all the elements of music, including broad expanses of high and low registers, multi-harmony, and timbre variations, are part of piano music, so the ear/brain processes and distinguishes compound auditory information simultaneously. Regardless of musical genre choice, whether classical or rock, or show and movie tunes, the elements are the same—rhythm, melody, harmony, timbre, dynamics, form—played with up to all ten fingers, in varied energies and styles, across a wide range of registers.

The type of instrument recommended is the *acoustic* piano (vs. electric keyboard)—the good old-fashioned 88 keys, in tune

I hope! The vibrations, energies, natural timbres, and muscular force required to play the acoustic piano will contribute more to the development of sensory and muscular development. A "real" piano is worth the investment, and there are many older pianos to be had. The instrument need not be a nine-foot concert Steinway baby grand! I began training (at the age of five) on an old upright piano until I was in college, when my family could afford to buy me a baby grand. And I went on to concertize! So the cosmetic value of an acoustic piano is not the consideration. Good used pianos are available, as long as they can be tuned, and there are any number of ways to research this, from instrument stores to online sites, to local shops, and thrift shops. *Oh, but we don't have room for a piano*, you say. My response: *Make the room, even if you have to use the piano as a dining counter!* The instrument on which the child will learn will be key to the progress and success of the training. At least I am not recommending a complete drum set—yet! (see later).

If an electric piano must be the choice, then it must be a *full-keyboard* (88 keys) with *touch-sensitive* mechanism, and a pedal. A touch-sensitive keyboard requires that to play loud more arm energy must be applied in order to press the keys down harder for louder tones, and vice versa. However, keep in mind that it is difficult for any child, let alone a spectrum diagnosed child, to go from home electric keyboard on which practice was done, to a teacher's acoustic studio piano. This can be a difficult and confusing transition, since the "feel" of the instrument is entirely different, as well as the sound and touch aspect. This may possibly cause, and has caused, distress and melt-downs in diagnosed students who often require sameness, or are unable to generalize information and instantly adapt to new circumstances. What's worse, if a child is practicing at home on a 65-key table-top electric keyboard, and has to adjust to the teacher's 88-key acoustic piano, where, now, is middle C? In addition, the auditory processing differences between an acoustic vs. an electric instrument, however slight they may appear to be, could be confounding to the brain's auditory system. I rest my case.

Stringed instruments for the beginner

Violin and cello

When instrumental training begins at a very young age (three to five years), then the other instrumental possibility would be a violin, although stringed instruments do not provide the same comprehensive brain-body-sensory development that the piano provides. The most popular stringed instrument is the violin, although the cello is often of interest to many children because of its deeper soothing tones, and the vibrations it yields.

Children drawn to the violin often begin training through the Suzuki training method that recommends commencing lessons at a very young age, through a rote-system of learning, with parental supervision of "homework" practice. This particular approach relies on *memory* and *tonal imitation* of recorded music that the student replicates, rather than through actual reading the music notation. And often parental supervision becomes a negative contribution rather than a support (we touch upon parental involvement in Chapter 6 "Lessons, Practice, and Penalties"). Such rote training can, of course, develop many areas of cognition, auditory acuity, and, especially, memory and imitation, along with contrasting motor planning of each hand, the left including fine-motor finger flexibility on the violin fingerboard, the right hand requiring muscular activities driving the bow across the strings. Training approaches depend on the abilities and cognitive level of the special-needs student. For some, this rote approach may be the only manner in which to achieve results; for others, a combination of rote and reading notation can be the better option. Consultation with an instructor is advised.

A cello is often the best instrument for an autism spectrum diagnosed youngster because of its deeper tones, and the fact that the instrument sits on the ground, leaning onto the body, providing sensual vibrations and proprioception information the brain enjoys. Fingering and bowing requirements are similar to violin, in that the left hand fingers are placed on the strings while the right hand draws the bow across the strings. The cello is held stable at the knees, so in effect, the whole body is involved in playing cello. If the child seems interested in its timbre, I often prefer cello to violin training, for the listed reasons. What's more, while the violin must be held under one's ear and beneath the chin, with the sounds penetrating immediately into the ear, this can cause auditory discomfort. The cello does not present the same issue, and may be more calming and comfortable. Various training methods, including Suzuki, exist for cello as well, so rote training, and/or reading notation may be part of that learning activity. Whether cello or violin, positive results can contribute to the ASD child's development.

As the student grows and enters regular school, many elementary school music programs begin instrumental lessons by 3rd or 4th grade, with stringed instrument classes and string orchestras. Sometimes band instruments become available by 5th or 6th grade, (discussed below). The age group for 3rd and 4th grades is between eight and nine years old, a bit older than my preferred starting age of three. Still, undertaking a stringed instrument in school provides an immediate social interaction—playing in and with a group. The piano generally does not provide such interaction. I recommend adding a stringed instrument to ongoing piano lessons, rather than making an either/or choice. This can easily be achieved, since the child who began piano several years earlier will, by 3rd or 4th grade, already be able to read the single clef line required for the violin. In that case, the student will be ahead and comfortable in the undertaking.

Caution: For a special-needs student in any school instrumental class, if behavior becomes problematic, it is recommended that the student participate in segments of time, rather than the entire 30-or-so minutes of the class. Ten-minute increments (also described in Chapter 6), followed by brief breaks, private review of information with the aide, and return to the class for the closing ten minutes, is enough for attaining the information, while reducing stress, possible melt-downs or other discomforts.

Whether considering violin or cello, it is important for the size of the instrument to be appropriately fitted to the student. With violins, a teacher or music store attendant will know how to fit the instrument according to the length of the relaxed but extended left arm of the student. (The usual measurement is for the instrument to be placed under the child's chin, with the left arm extending with a slight bend at the elbow, along the bottom of the instrument, reaching and cradling the top scroll with the hand. The hand surrounds the scroll, and the arm's elbow is just slightly bent, rather than straight.) For a cello, again special size measurements exist, which the instructors will facilitate to be certain the size is adequate for the size and build of the seated child. Accurate measurements of instruments are important in order not to over-stress arm positions (violin) or arm and leg positions (cello). Unlike piano lessons, where the instrument is always the same size (and the chair might need a cushion to raise the student a bit), with the violin and other stringed instruments, the sizes change with the growth patterns of the students, so there are continuous adjustments in fingering and playing of stringed instruments, according to the size of the instrument. This can become problematic with various levels of spectrum children, since it requires regulation of playing techniques with each new, larger instrument. (Another reason to continue piano, in addition to strings.)

A word about guitar and bass

Many 3rd and 4th graders are now aware of music genres involving guitars and basses, such as rock, jazz, country, etc., often also including strong rhythms and drums. The guitar, while an extremely suitable instrument to begin by ages eight or nine, is quite a bit more complex to learn than the violin or cello. The reason for this is that there are many ways of delivering sounds on a guitar, and these depend on more bilateral fine-motor involvement. While the left hand will finger the strings of a guitar, the right hand can either strum, with or without a pick, pluck, or finger strings individually to obtain chords or arpeggiated (rolling) sounds. On a violin or cello, one hand does the fingering, while the other slides a bow, so it's more a full-arm activity. On the guitar, both hands can apply finger techniques, but in different ways, since one hand will press down on the strings to change tones while the other hand's fingers will determine how the sounds are rendered. In addition, isolating two or three strings to pick or strum, among the six, can be a challenging task.

For a young child, I do not recommend guitar, but prefer to suggest that it be included, if desired, during the teenage years, when the hands and fingers are more substantially able to undertake the various techniques of guitar playing. Keep in mind, also, that there are different kinds of guitars, in various sizes appropriate to various playing styles. For instance, a classical guitar has a wider fingerboard, requiring strong and nice long fingers, wider hand extension, and more variety in right-hand playing techniques (less strumming, more individual finger work on individual strings, etc.). In the folk guitar, the fingerboard is a bit narrower enabling left hand multi-fingering pressing strings to create chords, while the right can strum with a pick, or play multi strings with individual fingers, etc. Then, too, there are electric guitars of various sizes, shapes, and colors, which teenagers prefer, and are certainly fun to learn because the sound is amplified. In general, the study of any guitar, from classical to electric, will depend on child's choice, age, and potential ability to navigate the instrument. Consideration of guitar would best be for a child of eight years and up, of course with instructor consultations.

The double bass is a very interesting stringed instrument that some spectrum children might prefer, perhaps after beginning on another stringed instrument. First, the lower pitches provide enormous vibrations and proprioceptive input to the brain about the body! In addition, the deep tones are very comfortably processed by the auditory system because the frequencies are slower than higher-pitched instruments. In school string classes and string orchestra, the bass is somewhat less active in the music—meaning, it may play longer tones, or fewer repetitive tones—and can be more accessible to negotiate by the student. One of my therapy clients began on the cello in the school string class, and after attaining much success on that instrument, decided he preferred the double bass—which is what he continues to play! So, instrumental training can progress from violin to cello, bass, guitar, and even viola. (The viola, a larger, heavier instrument than the violin, requires learning a different clef (the C clef), and due to the weight of this larger instrument, may be tiring to hold beneath the chin for extended periods of time.)

While an acoustic piano should be purchased as part of every home, a stringed instrument should be rented rather than purchased, because the student will quickly outgrow instrument sizes. Orchestral stringed instruments (violin, cello, etc.) are usually rented through schools or music stores. Guitars may need to be purchased, but since I recommend that guitar lessons begin in older ages, it may be that a child would take a bit longer to outgrow a guitar. Still, that may require initial investment followed by resale.

Woodwind and brass instruments

In my clinical practice, all my clients, young and old, must own a recorder—whether a soprano or an alto recorder. Part of the music-based treatment involves breath control for reduction of anxiety and stress. Any instrument that requires the breath will efficiently regulate the body's release of muscular tension, and anxiety! I recommend learning to finger and play the recorder first, before any other wind instrument is sought. It is not difficult to blow into a recorder. Fingering to cover the holes aids fine-motor control and tactile acuity, so learning to play recorder contributes to positive sensory input. Many schools begin music classes with learning to play recorder. Many simple children's tunes can be played on the recorder with little difficulty. Playing in tune is not especially problematic, and tunes are immediately recognizable. How well the child takes to playing recorder will determine whether another wind instrument would be a viable selection. The child's interest and choice will drive the decision.

Two wind instruments other than recorder are recommended for the younger beginner (in addition to piano, of course). One is the flute, but the ASD child may have difficulty at first pursing the lips correctly to direct the air across the instrument's opening. One way to encourage and "practice" this is by blowing across the top of a soda bottle. This is fun, and can be practiced by both child and parent as a game, using different size soda bottles (glass, not plastic) to produce different timbres and tones. Success may be slow in coming, but if the child's interest leans toward a flute, it is the most practical way of learning how to purse the lips and blow. Patience is required, which can also teach the child a bit about waiting, practicing, trying, and, ultimately, achieving. Once this begins to develop, the flute can be presented. Perhaps at first, just the top part of the flute can be presented for continuation of blowing practice. After a time, the remainder of the flute can be inserted. The flute instructor will guide the learning process. Perhaps rote learning for fingering and tones may be required, before note-reading, as mentioned above with stringed instrument learning. Breath control is an excellent way to attain behavioral control, so a wind instrument in addition to the recorder can play a leading role in sensory and behavioral development. By 3rd or 4th grade, the elementary school may have band instrumental training available, so that the youngster can participate in those classes.

Another wind instrument possible, though much more complex, would be the clarinet. However, that would require a great deal of interest and learning ability on the part of the child, because rendering tones on a clarinet is quite intricate and tiring. In addition, the clarinet requires reeds in the mouthpiece, and a younger ASD child may have difficulty with the task of tightening the reed to the mouthpiece, seeing to it that it is moist enough to vibrate, and then rendering a tone. If the child is higher-functioning, with good comprehension and organization skills, the clarinet may be enjoyable. I would consult with the band director, but also, know your child's abilities—not *dis*-abilities, but abilities—in order to make a decision that will not be stressful to you or the child. Other wind instruments I would not recommend (such as bassoon, piccolo, etc.) unless the student is quite high-functioning, able to be attentive to instruction, with good self-care abilities. I would just stay with either recorder, flute, or clarinet.

Brass instruments are fun—sometimes more fun than woodwinds, because bands include trumpets, trombones, and various horns. If band programs begin in middle school, the child may be able to undertake, and may prefer, a band instrument such as trumpet or trombone. I once had a client who preferred to learn the tuba! And he did. But that is rare, since tubas are a bit cumbersome. In any event, regardless of which brass instrument is undertaken, I suggest first that a mouthpiece (the part into which one blows) of the instrument of choice, is purchased, so that practice of blowing—again, pursing the lips in a certain way and having them vibrate into the mouthpiece—can be done at anytime, anywhere. The young lad who wanted to learn tuba had a tuba mouthpiece first, and was practicing how to blow and create sounds just into the mouthpiece before actually including the instrument itself!

For any brass instrument, I recommend discussing with the instructor how to purchase the mouthpiece and begin the process of strengthening the lips, pursing them correctly, and creating sounds with the lips vibrating.

Selection of a band instrument must be something the student desires or prefers. If there are no preferences, then consultation with the band instructor will be best.

In short, playing an instrument in the band is not only great fun but a major contributor to social skills development and team work! So if the school offers band, the parent must advocate for the ASD student to undertake the learning of an instrument. It may be a slow process, the student may not be "up to the rest of the group," but the instructor must find a way of including the student—as difficult as it may appear. Adaptive music scores, simplification of songs, etc., and other ways of including the student should be pursued, in the best interest of the student! Exclusion is not the answer!

Drums

I saved the topic of drum lessons for the last because drum instructors appear to have an age limit for when a youngster can begin drum training. That age seems to be around six years old, but preferably eight years of age. Although I don't agree with this restriction, it is inevitable that a parent will have difficulty employing a drum instructor for a younger-aged child. So, by the time the child is ready to begin drum instructions at the ripe old age of eight years, s/he will have had several years of piano lessons, during which time bilateral arm and sensory development will have developed nicely, so that use of bilateral parallel or alternating arm movements required in drumming will already be familiar to the brain.

In addition to piano lessons, drum training is the most highly recommended instrument for any child on the spectrum, or with any other diagnosis! Drumming provides the best multitasking, mind-brain-body interaction and physiological development of any instrument (aside from piano). Rhythm embodiment (entrainment) is a good solution to many sensory issues in autism, including proprioception, upper-body gross motor coordination, sequencing, task attention, and rhythmic organization of brain and inner body activities. As stated earlier, rhythmic stimulus creates rhythmic neuronal activity in the brain, resulting in paced and organized behaviors and cognitive thinking.

Piano training is replete with rhythmic information—pulse, pace, patterns—requiring arms and fingers to reproduce music in rhythmic sequences. If the youngster began with (or continues) piano, s/he is now very ready to undertake drum training successfully. While piano playing includes multitasking (arms, legs on pedals), plus multiple tonalities, harmonies, melodies, drumming includes all of the above, but purely through rhythm! Rhythm provides the neuronal drive for organized movement and behaviors! Timbres of various drums (bass drum, high hats, snares, cymbals, etc.) and very subtle drum tones contribute to auditory acuity, attention, memory for patterns, and multitasking (as on the piano). Two arms, and a leg thumping the bass drum, all coordinate to bring about rhythmic arm movement and drum patterns in various tempos, which keep the brain attending and focused. Upper-body muscle tone is highly increased in drumming, and various mallets contribute to flexibility in hand grip.

Rhythm notation is different than tonal notation, and a bit less complex to read. Notations indicating which drum or other percussion to play is often included, but the basic rhythmic notation is clearer, so learning to drum does not present many stressful issues and, in all, is highly recommended! Several of my therapy clients pursued drum lessons by various instructors, and the more training that was had, the more progress was made, both on the piano and in the therapy session.

I can hear you, the reader, shouting *But I don't want to hear that noise all day!* to which I say, simply *Get over it. Perhaps your ASD child is putting up with noise and stress all day, that he or she would like to avoid.* The child's bedroom is a safe environment to house a drum set for the home. Or the drum could sit near the piano, if other household members play, so that a home "band" can evolve. Or there are practice drum heads, and also electronic drum sets to which ear phones are applied (although I do not recommend those), that can alleviate "noise." Here again, as with the piano, I recommend and urge obtaining acoustic drums—in other words, the real thing. Acoustic auditory information is best, all around, for any instruments, with the exception, perhaps, of the electric guitar which is now very common.

Most middle schools have band programs, and playing drums in the band is great fun! School instruction in drumming can then be supplemented with after-school percussion training to further skills development. Parent must advocate for the student's participation in school band or orchestra at all times! As stated earlier, exclusion is not the answer.

En fin—in the end

I bring this chapter to a close with a repeated exhortation that parents of any children, but especially children that carry the diagnosis of ASD, Down, or ADHD, or any other issue, should seriously consider the positive impact of instrumental training—both for benefits in early childhood, as well as for positive function in later life. In order of preference, I recommend piano, *at a very early age* and onward, followed by including drumming. Stringed instruments, guitar, bass, brass, and woodwind instruments, especially if part of elementary school music programs, should be considered, because all students—especially diagnosed students—should be included in orchestra or band programs. The most practical instrument to begin with is the recorder, to teach the brain various breath controlling activities. But whether strings, wind, or other instruments are learned, piano and drums are best for developing whole-body rhythmic sensory integration and paced behavior, not to mention excellent auditory training.

In sections of Chapter 4 we discussed the process of engaging that special teacher and/or music-based clinician who will musically motivate and train the child, but the truth is that many instructors will not be comfortable undertaking the teaching of an instrument or voice to a special-needs student. In the end, the parent must be the child's *continual advocate*.

Meanwhile, *sing, sing, sing!*

CHAPTER 6

LESSONS, PRACTICE, AND PENALTIES

Graphic courtesy of Miriam Gallup Jones, age 15

Taking music lessons in order to attain an instrumental or vocal skill is quite an extraordinary activity. Unlike school studies that involve daily repetitive exercises and tasks supervised by classroom instructors, individual music lessons basically place students in a nearly no-win situation. Why?

To begin with, a *lesson*, that is, a meeting with the instructor, occurs only *once a week*, at most for one hour, and more than likely, just half an hour, depending on the age and abilities of the special-needs student. That virtually leaves the student (and parent) to his or her own resources for the remainder of a week, with the seeking of parental assistance essential to help recall, repeat and reinforce the instruction, *without the presence of the teacher or supervisor.* And, if parent is not musically experienced or trained, parental assistance is of little use. As a result, regardless of how diligent and astute the student is, the student is at a disadvantage, having to rely entirely on self-motivation, self-correction, self-discipline and recall of information, and/or parental participation in order to practice the skill according to instructions. The battleground is set!

Compared to training in academics and sports in which there is *daily*, third-party *supervised* instructional practice, the lonely music student is left to his/her own devices. Can you imagine students of tennis, baseball, football, basketball, or golf receiving only once-weekly coaching lesson, for just one hour at most, and having to practice unguided or at the urging of a parent who may or may not know the game? Unlikely!

For the music student, especially for the student with special needs, the parent or caregiver is in somewhat of an adversarial relationship, regardless of the extent of knowledge, background, or training in music the parent might have. In essence, the parent's role is that of being chief hatchet man and executioner on behalf of the teacher! To force or not to force practice? To push or not to push for results? To remind or reprimand? To stay out of, or move into, the situation? These are some of the questions! In financing the training, parents do have some vested interest in how well the musical development of the student is going, not to mention the expectation of positive returns in the form of pride and gloating. Often, the higher on the spectrum the student, the more such questions and battles increase, because higher ability and talent supersede *realistic* expectations.

To force or not to force—
that is the question

No! Forcing does not work, for any child, in any subject! For a special-needs youngster, the issue of achievement is often clouded by the diagnosis, but expectations are not often adjusted to accommodate particular needs or momentary moods. A gifted spectrum student whose innate personality is of an independent nature, ornery, unwilling to be directed by parent or teacher, can present disconcerting problems to both teacher and parent. Any skills training requires *practice*, and the need to practice for attaining various levels of proficiency, whether memorizing the multiplication table or practicing scales and musical compositions on a instrument, often creates problems.

So, the practice battles begin. *Did you practice today?... Go! Practice that piano!... Do as I say!*; and so on. Thence often several punitive behavior-modification elements ensue: *You can't watch your favorite TV program unless you practice first.... You forfeit your computer time because you didn't practice!... No, I won't take you to your favorite store until after piano practice... You won't have dinner unless first you practice...*; and so on. Furthermore, since most special needs students require some parental assistance, a parent must be prepared to clear time for joining in the student's practice activity. It's akin to a home-schooling situation. These are ingredients that ultimately can launch major melt-downs, by all parties involved, with shouts and screams, and evasions. *I don't like the piano!!... I don't want to practice!!... I want my treats!...*; etc.

In addition, students with language delays, who are unable to express their frustrations and dislikes verbally, will simply have tantrums and become inconsolable, and practice does not happen.

Surely this is not the optimum way to learn a musical, or any, skill. Is it any wonder that children want to quit music lessons? Anyone would, given the fact that it contributes so much psychological and emotional distress to the battlefield between parent and child. It cannot be any fun if it means many fights, outbursts, and parental disapprovals. *Ah, but s/he's so talented...*, you say. No. Forcing does not achieve the desired results, and will only create often lifelong animosities and emotional baggage, added to the already-existing stress factors. Here are some areas of consideration to ponder, discussed in detail in the following section, which provide some keys to success:

- attitude to and expectations about your child's music training

- commitment to helping your child continue through high school

- consistency in providing support for your child's practice routines.

Attitude and expectations

Why are you selecting music instruction for your child? What are *your* expectations for your child's success and joy? How committed are *you* to the continuation of training, if the student is less than a child-prodigy (or savant, to use my least favorite word)? Should lessons be discontinued? Is it worth the stress?

These are important questions to ask yourself before considering music instruction for your child. It is not enough to say *S/he's interested... S/he loves music and touches the keyboard all the time...* or *S/he's showing an aptitude.* Embarking on instruction of any discipline requires full, consistent, continuous commitment to the task, regardless of outcome. The question here is not whether the "stress is worth it" but rather what can be done so that there is no stress. Here, the contribution of the instructor to the learning process is important. Bottom line—the relationship between the student and instructor must be positive, and established from the outset. The parent should not be the "hatchet man" on behalf of the instructor. The student/teacher relationship, as in a school situation, must be such that the student works to satisfy the teacher's directives. The teacher takes it upon him/herself to indicate support, approval, suggestions, discussion (if possible) about the assignment so that the student understands that this undertaking is an assignment issued *by the instructor*—not the parent! The parent's role is simply to stand by, aid, and assist when/if needed, but never to assume a role as music instructor. Indeed, if a parent is well versed in music skills, the problem increases! *I heard a wrong note, do it again!... You're out of tune... You're not playing in rhythm...*; etc. It must be understood that the student should work to satisfy the teacher, first! Parent—stay out of it! Let the teacher teach.

Commitment

Music training, as with any other physical activity, is a *cumulative* process. By that is meant that information accrues and compounds upon previous information, accumulating to higher levels of knowledge and proficiency. Similar to learning an alphabet that leads to reading, writing, and comprehension, the language of music also begins with an alphabet, plus sensory and muscular coordination, developing into a level of proficiency for rendering the "reading and comprehension" of the musical task.

In short, music skills training is an *accumulation* of musical information and experiences, and is very well worth the journey. The window of opportunity for becoming rather proficient at any musical task may be narrow for a special-needs student (or anyone, for that matter), but *consistent continuation* is imperative for enhancing brain development and child growth. As with language learning, whereby some students grow up to become authors, poets, and playwrights, others are satisfied just being able to read the daily newspaper or best-seller, and to sign a greeting card. Regardless of levels of attainment, no one stops learning to read, write, or count until, at the very least, after high school!

Music skills training is no different! Once it is begun, it should become an educational commitment on the part of the parent, to have the student continue training at least until graduating from high school. *But why,* you ask, *if the child shows minimal talent, interest, or ability, should it be continued? After all, it is costly and quite time-consuming.* For a spectrum-diagnosed student, the importance of musical skills training cannot be stated too often, nor should it be underestimated. The discipline, the brain development, the task focus, the sensory and physical coordination, and attention to detail, the breath control (if studying a wind instrument), is unsurpassed by any other activity! Just the "stick-to-it-iveness" ability required in learning instrumental or vocal skills replaces any "therapy." What's more, the self-gratification of achievement of a skill, no matter how small it might be, is worth the battle! So if possible, yes, music training should be continued, in order to secure the ability to focus and organize behaviors through the discipline of music training; and your steadfast committment to the training will help the child continue.

The answer to fulfillment in musical training should *never* be contingent upon ability, interest, talent, or future professional potential. Music training is a discipline well worth undertaking for reasons well beyond "talent." Its value is documented in endless research studies indicating enhanced brain power, physical coordination, psychological self-discipline and self-awareness, positive sense of self-worth and satisfaction, creative self-expression, and much more, in persons who have had musical skills training, versus persons who have not. There is no reason to assume that this would differ in special needs students. The brain is being taught information, and thus is becoming more efficient in mind-brain-body coordination.

Consistency—routines and schedules

Music training is aerobics for the brain! Once the parent is committed to adding music training to a child's education curriculum, and willing to "stick it out," this attitude will enable the student to develop all the more efficiently. Such development may not be visible immediately but, indeed, later in the person's development, as research is indicating.

Consistency is the key word. Children with special needs especially need *sequential indicators and systematic regulations* that are consistent within the child's comfort zone. Students on the spectrum particularly prefer sameness upon which they can rely. This is similar to school programs that post schedules and sequences of activities in order to help spectrum students know *what's next*, with no surprises! I suggest several approaches here.

First, both teacher and parents might refer to the task as "homework" rather than "practice," since that is consistent with schooling requirements. I use, and have recommended the use of, the term "piano homework" (or "cello homework" or "flute homework", etc.). The term "homework" is more familiar to children, and also suggests the recall and repetition of information, actions similar to what is expected at school. The word "practice" is somewhat alien. We don't say "practice arithmetic" for the most part. We ask about arithmetic homework. Similarly, music "homework" has worked best with students that I have taught.

Second, instrumental (or vocal) homework time should not be measured by hours or minutes. Such designations have very little meaning for any student, let alone one with special needs. If told to practice for an hour, the student will sit for the hour, stare at the clock, fussing with the instrument, not knowing how to undertake "practicing" a task, rather than spending the required time at the instrument. Obviously this achieves very little. If a student is a quick-study, a one-hour practice session may be too much; vice-versa, if a student is a slow-study, a one-hour session may not be sufficient. It's not about the amount of time. It's about knowing how to spend the time! So instead, the teacher and parent should indicate how many repetitions of various tasks and sections of a piece, exercises, or scales are required to be done per sitting, and how many days of the week the "homework" is to be undertaken. This way, the student is actually taught how to practice. For instance, I direct my piano students (all students, diagnosed or not) to repeat a particular set of measures (or number of pages, etc.) four times (or three, or five, depending on level) per sitting of music homework, each day of the week, except Sundays, birthdays, and holidays.

Some students achieve quickly, others are slower. It is not a matter of "how long" to sit with an instrument, or how quickly to learn something, but rather *how many repetitions* of a task homework is required, and *how often* per week prior to the next lesson the homework must be undertaken. It is possible that the same assignment would be repeated for several weeks before being able to move further along. It is also possible that some assignments are so quickly learned, that more homework material might be required. This is for the instructor to determine. I had many special-needs students who would often negotiate with me (where possible), regarding *how many repetitions,* and *what days* the homework should be undertaken. This allowed the opportunity for the student to participate in his/her own approach to skills learning. Several students, including those on the spectrum, were able to take responsibility by being able to select their homework preference and approach, and to indicate the weekly procedure. I would ask *So, how many repetitions do you think you would need, or would be enough in order to tackle the task?* and/or *How many and which days this week will you be able to devote to this homework?* In this way, the student is directing his/her practice time, setting his/her own standards, with instructor approval. I notate the assignment, including number of repetitions and days, in the student's assignment book, and advise the parent *not to monitor the requirement,* but simply to answer questions the student may need clarified. In many instances, I was teaching the parent along with the child, in the event that the child would need clarification. The rest is up to the student and me, to be reviewed at the following lesson. From what I was told, this approach yielded no arguments! If the student did not comply, it was up to *me* to take further actions. Yes, there were many instances when the student entered unprepared, or complained and wanted to discontinue. In those cases, I would smile, accept that the material was not worked on, and proceed with eurhythmics rhythm activities and piano (or instrumental or vocal) improvisation. This, too, is the learning of a skill—the skill of self-expression through music!

Third, given the format of homework repetitions each day, sometimes I suggest separating the homework into daily individual segments, performing segments at different times of the day. For instance, with several students, I suggested X number of repetitions of task A after dinner, followed by X many repetitions of task B before bedtime, and, if possible, X many repetitions of task C in the morning before leaving for school. In other words, to avoid tediousness, and maintain a level of interest, the "music homework" need not be done all at one time. Pleasurable things in between can often divert anxiety and melt-downs. In addition, many special-needs young people have additional therapies and after-school activities, or siblings being transported to various activities, so music homework may not be executed in one sitting. Short periods of "practice," with breaks, snacks, water, are preferable to one long sitting! The brain tunes out after a short while, leading the way to fatigue and stress.

Fourth, yes, rewards do work! In any form of behavior management it is always beneficial to reward a student's achievements in some way. Just the sitting to do music homework, and repeating a task the assigned number of times, merits a reward of the parent's or student's choosing. But supportive words and love from the parent and siblings are the best rewards. Hearing a parent say *I appreciate that you did your work... I love hearing you play piano (or flute or tuba)...* and other encouraging words are the best behavioral rewards. It's not so much about being proud of achievement, more about being proud of an undertaking—proud of the doing, right or wrong, correctly or incorrectly! Words of encouragement go a long way to motivate while relieving anxieties and stress associated with skills learning. *Your teacher will also appreciate that you did the music homework this week.*

There are various approaches to reward systems, such as Practice Charts that receive checks for accomplished homework followed by Gold Star earned. I prefer that those not be used, since students have enough of such documentation at school. I prefer that the student is encouraged to achieve a level of self-gratification—the "I did it!" feeling, which, in and of itself, is a Gold Star self-reward!

Finally, select your words carefully so that there is little room for negative interpretations. For instance, if student resists doing the homework and you've previously said *I'm proud of your work,* might the student think you are no longer proud if s/he has not done the work?

Judging successes or achievements can be dangerous as well. *You've done a good job… or You play so well when you do the homework…* while it may make a child feel good in the moment, will it reverse when the homework was not done, leading the child to feel "not good enough" as a result? In short, all children are very sensitive to parental approval or rejection, and many comments can rebound negatively at a later time. Special-needs children are even more sensitive to approval or rejection. Therefore, using better terminology to describe the requirements for successfully achieving a particular skill, whether in music, sport, or academics, and carefully encouraging and motivating repetitions and "practice," will abate wars between parent and child. The parent's role is *unconditional* support. This must apply to any instructor as well. Chapter 4, discussing interview questions to ask when selecting a teacher or therapist, recommends what to look for and how to support the student/teacher relationship.

Review and some final thoughts

In music training, as in any other learning experience, the *relationship between student and teacher is of fundamental importance.* A student's motivation to succeed at a task, or even to please the adult, will often depend on the student's interest in *showing the teacher (or Mom) that I can do it!* Not because the parent shrieks! Not because the siblings are upstaged. Not always because the discipline of practice will be rewarded with extra TV, cookies, or treats. In large part, my adaptive piano students want to do well "for me," which of course translates into their own self-pride in achievement. Therefore, careful selection of a teacher is equal in importance to careful selection of the instrument, discussed in other chapters.

An instructor able to motivate a student will often prefer that the parent *not intervene*, so that student/teacher relationship can develop and attain positive interactions, rather than student/ parent battles. The point is to enable and *empower* the student into attaining the *self*-discipline to learn, regardless of the student's age! Too often a teacher will be more ambitious for the student than either the student or parent. Although this often can produce positive results, it can also become a detriment to learning, in addition to risking the positive relationship between student and teacher. Unfortunately, many instrumental instructors, often younger teachers with limited experience in addressing the psycho-emotional needs of youngsters, particularly special-needs students, tend to delegate the responsibility of practice supervision and repetition of instructional information to the parent in charge, immediately creating a potential battle between parent and child.

When my own child was learning an instrument, I was fortunate that each instructor specifically stipulated that I *not* participate in the learning process, *in any manner other than encouraging support and monitoring possible non-musical problems* (e.g., sitting incorrectly, not properly holding an instrument, etc.). Since I am a professional concert pianist, obviously this was going to be quite a challenge to my own self-discipline in staying out of the situation! However, as difficult as that was, I was confident that the instructor could indeed handle my child, and I trusted that the teacher/child relationship would bring about the practice discipline without my intervention. In fact, I usually preferred to be far from the practice arena. I was of the opinion that if the child were failing in her tasks, it was up to the teacher to take charge of the situation. That is what I was paying for! The child's failure would not be a transgression against me, her parent, but against the teacher's training requirements. My role in helping my child was to sometimes provide strategies for tackling certain technical difficulties (vibrato, etc.), but they were in the form of simple ideas rather than "teaching" the technique.

Let us consider some problems with certain currently popular training methods that require parental participation (e.g., Suzuki training). If the methods emanate from cultures outside of the U.S., it must be understood that parent/child relationships in other parts of the world are not at all similar to American culture, and that American children are raised differently than children in foreign lands. Therefore, attempts to import training systems from other cultures is to impact and perhaps completely change American family dynamics. To me, this is quite impractical! Not to judge certain methods in a negative way, one must consider the parent and family dynamics factor as potentially stressful and perhaps even detrimental to certain training. Methods that require parental participation by monitoring and supervising home learning and practice, or even attending lessons, can have unfortunate results and cause many wars at home.

For starters, parents are perhaps the most competitive species of humanoids on the planet! *My child's on Book 3 already. What book is your child on?... I don't have to tell my child to practice! She loves it! How about yours?... My child's on the spectrum, loves music, and has perfect pitch! How about yours?...*; and much more. I often could not understand why some instructors were accepting a full fee for lessons rather than sharing the fee with the co-teacher—the parent! It is felt that the child *must* succeed, not for his or her own "feel good about self" interest, but to please Mom and Dad! *Mom and Dad love me more...!* Of course this is a distortion! But a child does not understand that. The competitive nature of the parent, which translates into undue coercion and stress for the child to practice and succeed, can often create a major home front battlefield, and eventually cause the child to hate him/herself, the parents, and music.

In short, the training method, the instrument, the teacher, and the expectations must be carefully considered. Most often, these are neglected in the haste to seek music instruction. Music is important for any child, diagnosed or not. But careful considerations must be included in the undertaking, as described throughout this chapter.

Practicing an instrument or voice can really be a chore! Sitting at a piano for an extended length of time, or holding up a violin, or listening to an out-of-tune cello, or vocalizing nonsense syllables, or blowing into a horn, is definitely a test of endurance. Yes, it is not different from practicing back-hand strokes a thousand times, doing figures on ice for hours, slamming 500 baseballs back at a machine, looping baskets 100 times in a row, performing perfect back-flips over and over again on a gymnastic beam, or any other endurance discipline that one is attempting to master. Whether it's a scale on the piano, or a quadruple turn on the ice, *repetition is drudgery!* Boring. Stressful. Requiring inhumane levels of *patience*. What to do?

Several suggestions might be useful to consider. The parent and/ or instructor might objectively assess the potential of the student based on personality and learning styles, plus (a) ability to learn music; (b) potential for attaining certain levels of proficiency; and what those levels might be; (c) the purpose of musical instruction; (d) expectations held by teacher, parent, student; (e) commitment to staying with the program, regardless of challenges presented; and any combination thereof.

Once music instruction is introduced, regardless of ability and talent, a *commitment to "stick it out"* must be made by all parties involved. If music instruction is carefully introduced as part of a child's educational curriculum, regardless of potential, it should continue throughout his or her school years. It is no less important to obtain the discipline of learning through music, which has been known to enhance brain power, eye-hand coordination, physical coordination, language, and many other human adaptive functions, than it is to learn math or science. And just as it would not be an option to drop math or science based on difficulty or lack of talent, so it should not be an option to drop music training! It's value is incalculable. Too often, music training is dropped if a student does not plan to become a "concert" artist. Nonsense! I did not plan to become a mathematician or scientist, yet I had to endure more than ten years of math and science courses until high school graduation.

As a parent I, too, erred on the side of confrontation regarding practice. But when I was confronted with the possibility of eliminating music instruction from my child's life, I chose to remain committed to sustaining it as part of her educational curriculum, to be dropped only upon completion of high school, should that be desired. Until then, it was simply an additional course for study. Period. Achievement or failure was in her control. But practice or not, the training would remain. With that in mind, a daily calendar of activities was created, which is also something I recommend to all my students, and very especially to students on the autism spectrum who depend on systematic structure! From wake-up, breakfast, school, after-school, free time, through dinner, academic and music homework, TV, et al., the grid listing activities and approximate time slots was clipped to the refrigerator. As my child progressed throughout the day, activities were checked off as having been completed. Yes, there was flexibility—not much, but some—to enable special activities such as parties, overnight guests, trips, illnesses, fatigue, special school projects, "day off" rewards, and so on.

The discipline of homework included music. In effect, it was violin (or piano) homework. Yes, there were rewards for each element. For instance, academics were rewarded with various other activities of choice; music practice was rewarded with acquiring items of choice; chores for allowance dollars; and so on. (Penalty should not be part of the routine!) As a parent, and as a professional musician myself, I did, on many occasions, err on the side of supervising music practice from a distance (*I hear a sloppy passage, please repeat it!* and so on). I was always frustrated by the fact that her coach was not there on a daily basis to monitor the work instead of my having to confront the problem and create parent/child animosity! Music is the only performance "sport" that meets with the "coach" just once a week, as stated above, unlike gymnastics, tennis, skating, and other activities that meet with coaches at four or more times per week, if not daily. Still, when carefully considered, I exerted enormous self-discipline in remaining out of the situation unless my assistance was sought by my child.

It is possible to establish good practice habits. What a child fears most is parental animosity and rejection. Therefore, setting up work systems and schedules, especially those established with the help of the instructor and perused at the lesson, will go far in developing self-discipline for music homework. Always a student should be aware that the parent or caregiver *understands the drudgery* and necessity of the homework. Also, the student must fully understand parental commitment to "stick with it" regardless of struggle. As music instruction becomes part of a child's learning curriculum and self-discipline, it will eventually take its place among positive contributors to brain, sensory and motor development, attention and learning habits, and a level of self-discipline. It will never be a waste of time!

To conclude let me repeat that the discussion in this chapter is focused on understanding how to develop positive attitudes and self-discipline for good practice habits in music skills training while eliminating the need for hostility and punitive actions. The elements presented should be applied to any undertaking, whether music, academics, or sports, in order to gain positive benefits. In most cases, the benefits derived may not become obvious until many years later in the development of the student. Often, positive results do not make themselves immediately apparent. The special needs student may or may not become a professional musician; the student may or may not become technically proficient on the instrument or voice, regardless of hours of hard work; the student might not fully enjoy the experience. Never mind! But when the parent and instructors think *beyond the spectrum of abilities*, and understand that *consistency* and *continuity* are benefits, regardless of how these manifest themselves in later grown-up years, the student facing the challenge of learning an instrument will definitely reap the rewards!

CHAPTER 7

TAKING YOUR CHILD TO A CONCERT

I recently attended a piano recital in which part of the audience was seated on the stage surrounding the pianist, while the remainder were seated in regular theater seats beyond the stage. A woman and her five-year-old, rather  hyperactive, autistic son arrived seeking her seating location on the stage. She had specifically purchased tickets for stage seating, preferably in the first semi-circular row, close to the piano, so that her son, who loved piano music, would be able to observe the performer closely. Before beginning the performance, the pianist spent some preliminary time talking to the audience, then returned to the piano and began playing a Rachmaninoff Étude, rather energetically and fortissimo. The artist was performing on a 9-foot Steinway—a concert grand piano with an enormous dynamic range.

During the pianist's preliminary discussion with both the on-stage and off-stage audience, the child was becoming fidgety and restless, with excess vocalization. During this behavioral display, the parent tried to subdue and quiet the child. By the time the pianist began to play, the child was in the process of moving toward a melt-down state, shutting his ears, shouting his discomfort, and attempting to flee. The parent could do very little to subdue the behavior, and they ultimately left the stage (yes, while the pianist was playing) to sit in the hall with the rest of the audience. However, the child's melt-down persisted and progressed to a level that the parent could not redirect. In short, the child could not be quieted. Finally, a concert official asked the woman to remove the child from the concert hall, in the interest of other attendees. The woman took the child and departed, but was very upset with the concert management and sent a rather insulting letter to the officials requesting a refund, decrying the manner in which it was all handled. How would you have handled this situation, as a parent, or as a concert official?

The world is a very difficult environment in which to navigate sensory stimulation for a person on the spectrum, especially a young child who harbors any number of sensory sensitivities and needs! The planet is not a quiet place. Sound is everywhere! Visual stimulation is abundant. Chatter is everywhere. Tactile issues exist and often are difficult to endure, such as clothes rubbing against a chair also stimulating one's skin, hard seats, hot or cold environments, and more. Noise is everywhere—fans and heating or air conditioning noise buzzing and coming on and off in rhythmic cycles, persons coughing or sneezing. These are difficult conditions for any child to accommodate, let alone a child on the spectrum. A restricted environment, such as a theater or concert hall, presents further potential discomforts. No one likes being asked to leave a performance, but where and with whom does the responsibility lie? An audience member with a persistent cough that disturbs other attendees is not asked to leave! (We hope that person will voluntarily leave until the cough subsides.) Should the parent here have waited to be asked to temporarily withdraw, or should she have undertaken that responsibility herself? Indeed a difficult question, and surely there are many opinions and answers that we will not debate here.

Prelude to a live concert

Exposing children, whether diagnosed or typically functioning, to the world of live concert performances is a very special learning adventure. Unlike various other cultural activities, the world of concert music has few "tour guides" to explain and usher children through the experience. Let's look at what it means to attend a concert.

Music, as we know, does not require semantic interpretation. It is an innate human instinct and need, understood by the brain without prior knowledge, which begins early in life, continuing throughout most of it. What, then, is *concert attendance* about, and how can a child on the spectrum, or any other child with sensory issues, sustain him/herself during a performance? In recent years, there have arisen various attempts to help quell some of the sensory anxieties inherent in a public event. From time to time, there are concerts advertised as being "Sensory Friendly," at which the music is tempered in volume, sound-regulating earphones recommended or distributed, and seating arrangements organized in more accommodating positions. Some movie theaters have begun advertising "Autism Friendly" film presentations, with which I am not especially familiar.

In reality, the natural planet is not a *sensory friendly* environment, and I prefer to help the growing sensory system to adapt to the natural environmental circumstances, when possible, rather than to superficially and temporarily accommodate attendance comfort. This is my personal opinion, and can be further explored at another time. Advocates for sensory-friendly events declare that if a venue provides earphones for persons with hearing problems, and if special seating or space is reserved for wheel chairs and other physically incapacitating circumstances, then why not have special accommodations for persons with other special needs? Perhaps. Since sensory issues are so abundant and diverse, no one remedy will be sufficient. For instance, the condition called *misophonia*, a sensory aversion to common sounds people make, such as sneezing, chewing (as in popcorn), paper rustling, lip smacking, and so on, actually has no accommodating remedy. In such cases, some form of sound-reduction earphones could be helpful. The jury is out on the use of earphones; however, in many cases, some adequate *prior preparations* for attending an activity merit investigation and consideration. What factors are involved in concert attendance?

First and foremost, a concert (or any other live theater experience) is about a person sitting in a more-or-less uncomfortably upright seat, staring at a stage of one or more musicians who are flailing arms at odd-shaped instruments with strings, blowing into shiny metal or dark wooden instruments, pounding on percussive instruments and piano, all addressing auditory and visual systems head on! *Attention span and sensory overload* are the first behavioral issues to be addressed at a concert. Any child, diagnosed or not, experiences the same problems. How long can anyone—let alone a special needs child—remain quiet, attentive, and relaxed when presented with such a surge of visual/auditory goings-on on the stage? This sensory assault, along with the comings and goings of audience members climbing over others or moving about, coughing, sneezing, snoring, entering or leaving, feet shuffling, heels clacking, and so much more maneuvering, is virtually a tsunami of sensory information. Is it reasonable to expect *any* child to "attend" and endure such sensory confusion and sit still for any length of time? Hardly!

Even adults squirm and move about in their seats, rustle their programs, yawn, and otherwise have trouble focusing, for the duration of the performance. For anyone at a concert, attention will wander in and out of the music being presented. This is true for any adult, especially for children, and most especially for special-needs children and those on the spectrum. Parents (or concert escorts) must be prepared to anticipate and expect this, and assume all responsibilities involved therein. Children receive information in many ways, not necessarily involving "paying attention" directly. One should *be prepared to accept* that a child may squirm in the seat, fiddle with the program, attempt to speak, ask for a drink or a nature stop, and behave in many other ways that adults often consider disruptive, intrusive, unacceptable, or as indicators of a child's diagnosis, or boredom, and discontent. But in fact, *such behaviors do not necessarily imply that a child is not paying attention!* It could mean, among other things, that the auditory-sensory-mental systems are (for the moment) on overload, requiring momentary escape to rest and reconfigure the processing patterns. And that's okay!

Listening and hearing are not synonymous! We *hear* all the time. We receive auditory/visual and other sensory information on an ongoing basis, without especially listening to (focusing attention upon) specific sound information. But *listening* at a concert, and helping children enjoy and learn from the listening experience, requires some diligent homework on the part of the parent. Do not just go in "cold turkey"! In order to help children benefit fully from a concert experience and *listen to* what they are hearing, you—the parent or concert escort—might do the homework that could also help *you* appreciate what *your* brain and sensory systems will experience during a concert.

What to do before concert day

Just listening to musical sounds in a concert is a unique, albeit rather difficult, experience. There are no cartoons, characters, or actions on which the visual sense can retain focus while listening, other than the dramatic body movements of the musicians. This is quite different from hearing music on a CD, or music in cartoons and commercials. Such music is generally in the *background*, not meant for focused hearing. In order for any child to learn how to bring music into the *foreground* at a live performance, some creative adult interventions and suggestions are necessary to stimulate different imagery. This can be a highly unique, and very rewarding experience. Once your children unleash their own imaginations, observing how music is being made and performed, they will often seek more of such auditory-visual experiences. Looking at how music is rendered increases auditory acuity of sound reception. In short, one hears better when one sees how the sound is produced. Such experiences increase auditory attention, in the long run.

Know your child! Know his/her habits, likes, needs, behaviors, sensory needs, and so on, and proceed to develop actions that will accommodate the child, beyond the ASD persona! If your child has never attended a live concert before, you must orient him/her to some expectations. If there are extensive sensory issues, and an inability to sit still or communicate needs in forms other than vocal, or your child has a tendency toward melt-downs, you must first *practice concert attendance* at home! "Cold turkey" attendance is neither efficient nor effective for any child, let alone a fearful special-needs child given to sensory overload. Some of the following steps can assist in preparing for the concert experience.

• Auditory orientation:

First thing to undertake relative to the upcoming concert event is to *introduce lots of music in the background, at medium to louder volume, every day, everywhere throughout the house,* so that the auditory system and brain begin to adapt somewhat to a sonic external environment. Talk and chatter, cough, make other noises, over the music background. Along with such distracting actions, do some movement activities mimicking musicians' actions (pretend to play piano, or violin, etc.) and have the child also imitate pretending to be an instrumentalist or vocalist. Undertaking such activities, while music is playing, will provide the brain with options regarding what to expect in an actual concert setting, how things will occur, and much more. In short, create a musical auditory environment, preferably with the types of music that will be presented at the concert, but any music (preferably non-verbal) will serve the purpose.

• Obtain concert information:

Phone the organization or concert office that is presenting the program to which you plan to take your child, and ask for seating arrangement, size of venue (big means big sounds, for instance), and any pertinent information that might be available that describes the music to be presented on the day you are attending. Often you will be able to *obtain program notes and descriptions of pieces* in advance. If you know your child's behaviors and interests well, you will also know the questions you need answered. In addition, when phoning the concert office, inquire about:

- information on the numbers and types of instruments likely to be participating—full orchestra or chamber size; soloists; concert grand-sized piano, any specialty performers, speakers, vocalists, choir, etc.
- pertinent or unique aspects of the program that can help you prepare your child for the experience (e.g., dance, visuals, intermissions, etc.)
- length of individual works; total expected length of concert
- work(s) they would recommend for preview prior to attendance (e.g., avant-garde pieces that might be odd to hear, loud music, fast, slow, etc.).

Armed with some pertinent information, you are now ready for your next pre-attendance tasks. The following is recommended:

- obtain recordings of some of the works being performed: libraries usually have tapes or CDs; the concert office and/or your child's school music teacher could direct you to obtaining the recorded music; some recordings may be available online (MP3s and YouTube), along with information on artists.

- Hold practice concert attendance sessions in your home:

  This can be fun, involving other typically functioning siblings and members of the family, and should be done at least one week or more prior to the actual concert attendance. Here's how to practice concert attendance:

  ○ Select a special time of day when family and friends can gather to "attend a home concert." Concert videos (YouTube) are best, since concert attendance is also a *visual* experience, and children can observe the music-making. Set upright chairs in theater style, in front of the TV or music medium. All speakers should be working—surround-sound home theaters are best, but if not available, some additional speakers set up will work well. The objective is to infuse the environment with sound, since that will be the atmosphere of the live performance. Turn the lights down (or off), take a moment to be quiet, then begin the "concert."

  ○ Find aspects (from the information you obtained) that will enable the child(ren) to "tune in" and listen to the flow of sounds. (Is the music loud, soft, fast, slow, dance-like, march-like, nervous, exciting, boring, scary, moody, etc.?)

  ○ Suggest *listening with eyes closed*, imagining the shapes of the movement and flow of sound (moving up and down or staying in one place, or being repetitive, etc.). The more your child accumulates associative information, the better will be his/her ability to sustain behavior and attention when at the live performance. Thinking beyond the spectrum here is very important. It's not about autism, but about the child inside, that can be brought out in this experience. Shutting down one or more sensory systems will help!

◦ *Applaud loudly*, when music is over! Some ASD children do not like the sound of audience applause, and this could bring about an in-concert melt-down, so applaud often and loudly, in order for a level of adaptation to this action to take place.

◦ Have an "intermission" during which you can review and make up stories about the music, bring attention to the volume of the music, the instruments being heard, how they are played and how many of an instrument can be heard, imitate being the performer or a pretend ensemble (everyone takes part in this), color or draw to describe the music, and so on. Have a brief snack and water (or juice), and return to the "concert."

Concert attendance practice should be repeated daily if close to the concert date, or weekly and as far in advance of concert date as possible. Select one musical work per concert practice, talk about it, then "attend." In effect, you are training the brain and sensory systems to anticipate and accommodate the experience as well as possible.

Holding practice concert attendance together at home where replay is possible, can be fun, educational, and terrific preparation for the actual concert hall experience. It can also instill concert behaviors, such as not talking while music is playing, developing various acceptable forms of non-verbal communication (e.g., arm movements indicating a need to go to the bathroom, or take drink, or leave).

Of course, there are times when concerts are a last-minute impulse activity allowing no time for prior preparation. However, if your children have experienced *any* form of prior preparation relative to previous concert attendance, they will recall, or can be reminded of, general aspects of concert attendance behaviors, such as sitting still and *focus listening,* that can then be applied to an impromptu situation.

At the concert

The experience described at the beginning of this chapter defines an episode that could have been averted, had some pre-concert preparation been undertaken by the parent. Parents of ASD and other special-needs children are usually very knowledgeable about their child's expected behaviors and problems in certain circumstances, especially public situations, and should be well prepared to take certain actions in the interests of both the child and others. A screaming child at a theater or concert hall is surely disruptive to other audience members, just as talking in a movie theater is disruptive to viewers. But if the child's behaviors cannot be appeased in some manner, should s/he continue in the very situation that may actually be contributing to the melt-down? A situation that is negative to everyone? Perhaps not. A sensitive parent will not await a directive from a concert official asking for the child to be removed. It goes without saying that remaining in the environment that is precipitating certain responses is a no-win situation for everyone. However, if a parent is well versed in redirecting the child's reactions and behaviors and has taken actions to prepare for the circumstance, there are ways to accommodate the needs to the benefit of all involved. There are a few behavioral expectations for young children attending a theater or concert performance. These may be a bit more intense with spectrum youngsters, but, in general, disruptive behaviors can be expected occasionally from any child, typically functioning or otherwise, since all youngsters have levels of impatience, boredom, and sensory inefficiencies.

Where to sit; how long to remain; what behaviors to expect

The first mistake made by the parent described at the beginning of this chapter was to ask for stage seating! If the mother knew her child's sensory and social sensitivities, she would have asked for theater seating, at the left side of the auditorium (from where the child could still have an unobstructed view of the pianist performing), in the first or second row, at the end of the row near the exit. The view would be close enough for the child to see, but the 9-foot concert grand piano sound would go more directly back through the center of the hall. This could have reduced auditory distress, if that were an issue, while still providing visual interest and curiosity. In addition, given the age of the child, short increments of attendance, with brief temporary exits to organize, could also have averted the anxiety.

In general, when taking children to concerts, it is very important, for the benefit of all involved, to carefully *consider seating arrangement, and length of attendance time.* Center seating with a hyperactive child is obviously undesirable! Aisle seating at a side section of the auditorium, close to an exit, is most practical for many children, and especially for spectrum children who may need quick temporary escapes. Side exits are preferable to having to run the length of a center aisle to leave. Also, side sections of an auditorium have fewer seats to be reached by late-comers who may need to climb over you to find their locations!

Concert behaviors of children vary greatly, according to age, concert experience, whether typical or diagnosed, and so forth. A concert-goer might consider shortening attendance time to a minimum, if he or she is anxious about the child's ability to sustain appropriate behavior throughout the length of a performance. If pieces are short, perhaps one or two works might constitute enough of the experience. Brief respites between works is recommended. Perhaps an entire one or more hours of music is overwhelming (to anyone), therefore having learned the child's limits as suggested above, the parent can determine when enough is enough. Some general behavioral considerations may be anticipated, as follows:

- Expect your child to squirm, become somewhat restless, look about, have sudden unrelated thoughts, and engage in other usually unacceptable public concert behavior. Don't forget they are still young and practicing attention techniques. *Be prepared.* Bring a small pad, crayons, ask the child to draw the sounds or images of the music; select a favorite person or instrument on stage to observe; observe the conductor's choreographic interpretation of the music; use earphones if preferred, to modify external sounds; bring a picture book of musical instruments for the child to leaf through if "bored," a small snack to chew (not chips or crunchy foods that make noise), definitely a small water bottle, (which can immediately redirect behavior), and more.

- Allow your child to respond with laughter, rhythm tapping, pointing to things, etc. Too many parents and teachers are eager to boast "perfect concert behavior" at the expense of genuine, naturally responsive reactions to the music! Everyone, adult or child, responds differently to audio/visual sensory input. It is beneficial to keep in mind that no two persons perceive sensations in the same way. Children included! Let the child squirm if needed. Don't be self-conscious about how your child is sitting, where the attention is, etc. Allow some of these behaviors to occur so that subsequently tantrums can be limited or avoided. And don't assume the child is not "attending" just because he or she prefers to sit under the seat!

- Prior to entering the hall, during intermission, and at the end of the concert, *recall and review* the home "practice concerts" and interesting facts that were shared in preparatory home listening activities.

Special considerations

As stated earlier, if you know that your child may not be able to "attend" throughout the full length of the concert—as is likely for special-needs as well as "typical" children and the very young—you may opt to attend just a portion of the concert; *half-hour or less* would be more than sufficient for a first-time experience, if a child is unable to sustain for longer periods. Also as suggested, you might request seating on the aisle or close to an exit should you need to make a quick escape. However, do not be too eager to extract the child from the experience due to "behavior" issues, unless it becomes truly intrusive and unbearable. Keep in mind that you are your *child's advocate*, not the guard of conformity. Your child will experience the concert in his/her own individual manner and, short of screaming and violence, *most conduct is acceptable.* Remember, too, that concert attendance is a theatrical experience! Everything becomes part of the drama and distraction, including audience behaviors, entrances, exits, coughs, sneezes, dropping or fiddling with programs, shuffling feet, and the like. For spectrum children with anxieties and fears, being in crowds is problematic, and such external audience occurrences and noises can be scary, further contributing to insecurities, anxieties, and behavioral melt-downs.

Keep in mind that a child's behavioral meld-down is less bothersome than the more distracting behaviors of the parent yanking, pulling, shushing or otherwise trying to subdue a child during a concert! If you are seated appropriately, you can unobtrusively exit with the child for a few minutes of recomposing, toileting, drinking of water, walking to release excess energies, crying if necessary, subduing the melt-down. In such cases, I recommend a ten-minute "recess," giving the child the option of either returning to the concert, or leaving entirely. Shrieking at, or physically manipulating the child will only escalate the tantrum and not result in positive or effective redirection!

Conclusion

In sum, there is no single "right way" for any child to attend (or pay attention at) a concert. Music moves people; people tap their toes or hands, sway or bob their heads, hum, smile, even snore. Music elicits emotions, and this may be a difficult, new sensation for any child, and especially for a child on the spectrum. Without experience in detecting and understanding sensations occurring within one's body, communication presents itself as "acting out." This is true for any child, not reserved only for a special-needs child.

This is why concert attendance practice is useful. Emotions and sensations can be identified in the safety of home, and expressed in positive ways.

Concerts are dynamic experiences for any attendee. Eyes flit back and forth across the stage, as if observing a tennis match, scanning the actions from which music emanates. Children cannot be expected to do otherwise! They, too, have their unique ways of experiencing music—and these may not conform to the expected norms of others.

Finally, live concerts are the best ways to enjoy and learn about music. Observing music being rendered is the best way to *hear* music. Live concerts are a total, whole-brain, whole-sensory experience, beyond just listening to a CD. But no one can say for certain how, or when, the concert experience will have an impact on the listener. It might be in-the-moment, or months, even years, later. Make no assumptions. "Not looking *at*" does not necessarily mean "not listening *to*" or hearing. Having a melt-down does not mean lack of interest, or even sensory discomforts, but rather, can be attributed to any number of body sensations and mental anxieties. If a parent is careful about securing appropriate theater seating, and undertaking the pre-concert homework described above, the child—*any* child—will have an extraordinary experience. Simply do *your* job, prepare yourself and your child for the experience, and then enjoy the concert. Your child's sensory systems and brain will definitely learn to adapt to auditory information! You will reap rewards!

PART THREE

ADDITIONAL CONSIDERATIONS

CHAPTER 8

MUSIC AND EXCEPTIONAL NEEDS

Happiness lies in the joy of achievement and the thrill of creative effort.

FRANKLIN D. ROOSEVELT

Musically gifted and diagnosed

"My Asperger child is a genius on the French horn! He wants to pursue music as a life's profession! But I don't want him to become a professional musician. He'll starve! Help!"

Several chapters have touched upon the possibility that a child on the spectrum, or with any other diagnosis, may have excellent aptitude and talent for learning a musical instrument, and should be encouraged to continue music training. Although the reader may have encountered this discussion elsewhere in this book, I feel it is worthy of repetition and review. I am always frustrated by the fact that for a child on the spectrum, the term "prodigy" is not used. Instead, we hear that the child has "splinter skills" or is a "savant." The fact is, whether the child is on the spectrum, or diagnosed with any other characteristics, the child can still be a "prodigy"—a high achiever at a skill, whether mathematics, science, technology, music, or other!

I have encountered many parents and caregivers concerned about the future survival ability of their diagnosed child who happens to display specific talents. As I state several times, my advice had often been sought regarding this, and my response has always been the same: *Your child might "starve" at any other employment or profession, whether technology, accounting, law, medicine, or sales!* In short, there is no guarantee for anyone that a particular profession is better than another. The important thing to consider is how content and comfortable individuals are with their work! Here the question is whether or not *any* employer in any profession will employ and accommodate a person on the spectrum, or someone with any other diagnosis, who is skilled in a particular endeavor! This is a question for society to answer, and everyone can do his/her job to change negative thinking in this regard. Many diagnosed young persons, who function high on the spectrum, or are diagnosed with ADHD, or Down syndrome, or with any other alternative abilities, and who have excellence in musical skills, can (and should) be able to pursue a successful career in music—from instrumentalist, to music instructor at any level, to university professor, to clinician, and more!

There are many examples of such achievements. Unless the reader/parent/caregiver has the power to predict the future, it is absurd to pre-judge who and how anyone will succeed or fail at any undertaking, let alone as a musician. Yes, one can suppose that a "day job" with a steady income, might be preferable to one in which auditions, travel, multiple interviews, competitions, built-in job insecurities, and other such related circumstances in the performing arts professions, appear to be less desirable, and imply more struggle than a simpler desk job. But what are we talking about here? Are we trading an achiever's talents, potential personal happiness, preferences, and enthusiasm for "security"? Furthermore, is there such a thing as "job security" in any profession, with any ability? Maybe. But I have always suggested that the only secure profession is that of undertaker (not meaning this as an insult to undertakers). Everything else is illusion of security.

Here again, as I have been suggesting all along through this book: *A diagnosis does not preempt talent and skill!* If your son or daughter displays excellence and talent in his/her musical studies, on any instrument or voice, and if there is commitment and adoration for music and music interactions, and if his/her various instructors deem the talent to be indicative of potential future professional engagement, as possibly a lifelong endeavor, then my answer is: *Let it go forth... go for it!* That is not to say that some back-up training education, as, for instance, in the field of music teaching, might not be advisable to include in one's studies, for those "rainy days." The more training in, and application of one's musical gift, the better prepared the musician is to adapt to related professions.

Areas of possibilities within the music profession abound, in this age of STEM (Science-Technology-Engineering-Mathematics), to which I add Music in STEM: Science-Technology-*Education-Medicine*. Beyond becoming a member of an orchestra or band, some promising professional areas include: Music in Medicine and Therapy; Music and Scientific Exploration, such as Neuroscience and Brain Function; Music and Technology, a continually expanding area of creative sound invention; Music Composition, yes, believe it or not, a lucrative area of music, especially for creating film scores using electronic technology, or music "needle-drops" for TV and radio commercials (a needle-drop is a 10- to 30-second music clip backing a commercial, as if the record needle is simply dropped onto a short piece of music).

Many musicians, educators, composers, instrumentalists, with various diagnoses (ASD, Tourette's, synesthesia, ADHD, physical incapacities, etc.) have achieved great results and rewards in their chosen music profession! One's talent never ceases to rear its head. One of my dearest former clients and piano students, a young man with extreme visual impairment (blindness) and various related sensory delays, who adored creating weird, unusual sounds on various instruments in my studio, is now an adult hired to develop electronic needle drops for extremely exotic videos and TV commercials! In fact, compared with his two non-diagnosed siblings, he is, in fact, the most financially successful—through music! Bottom line, I repeat: *A diagnosis does NOT preempt talent and skill!* Caregiver fears should be withheld in order to assure that the music student does not sense parental doubts, leading to the student's own doubts and fears. Many of my colleagues who are diagnosed on various levels of the autism and Asperger's spectrum have extremely successful music careers as university faculty, school music teachers, performers, music-based clinicians, authors, composers, and so on. Do not discourage the gifted student from pursuing his/her love of music. At the risk of repeating myself, I encourage readers to set fears aside and encourage music training.

Of course, some limitations to a career in/through music may present in autism spectrum music students. The main area of these setbacks might be the lack or limitation of verbal communication. This deficit obviously could limit teaching opportunities that require interactive expressive language. Nevertheless, there are always ways to communicate, and music is basically a non-verbal form of communication. The spoken language issue is not limited to ASD or other diagnosed populations. Many highly professional "typically functioning" musicians have difficulty with verbal self-expression, perhaps as a result of extreme shyness, lack of knowledge of the country's spoken language, or simply inability to produce coherent explanatory sentences. Fortunately, science and technology play active roles in decreasing these problems. So no, there are very few limitations to becoming a musician, if interest, talent, and student teachability is present. At the start of this section, a mother indicates that her ASD child is an excellent French horn player. Obviously that student has been "teachable," displaying talent, interest, and desire. That is enough to support musical training. The future remains to be seen.

Auditory and visual obstacles

Auditory

Music provides acoustic sensory stimulation processed through the *auditory* system, and throughout the whole body. In addition, learning to read music notation involves visual processing coordinated with the auditory, motor, and memory systems across many areas of the brain. Possible inefficiencies in these sensory collaborations are not limited to the ASD population, but are also visible in many ADHD, Down syndrome, and trauma diagnoses, as well as in many typically functioning youngsters. However, despite these deficits, children are enticed and drawn to music, and I encourage interactions with musical sounds and instruments. These interactions will eventually help the brain develop strategies with which to process and navigate incoming sensory information and motor control.

But my child, in addition to other diagnoses, is deaf. How would music work for her?—For persons in whom deafness is co-morbid

KIDS, MUSIC 'N' AUTISM

(co-existent) with other functioning diagnoses, there are various types of interventions, such as cochlear implants, and other devices that actually do enable "hearing" at various levels of processing. Being "deaf" is not a disability, and does not need to inhibit a child's learning or interaction with music. International percussionist Evelyn Glennie is a perfect example of a highly successful professional musician who is profoundly deaf.

In addition to deafness, there are varieties of lesser-known auditory deficits, such as *misophonia*, a condition that produces extreme anxiety, fear, and stress upon hearing particular sounds. These sounds could range anywhere from simply hearing the hissing of the wind, to a vacuum cleaner buzz, to a person's jingling of keys, or tapping a pencil on a desk, or chewing gum, and more. In diagnosed persons, the *misophonia* condition could be part of deficient auditory processing, and music could potentially alleviate this condition. (It is difficult to diagnose this problem in anyone, and a non-verbal child would clearly be unable to explain the issue to a medical professional or parent.) If *misophonia* is suspected, a consultation with a music therapist or teacher could provide insight to redirecting, decreasing, or perhaps even eliminating such problems. *Misophonia* has, to my knowledge, not hindered interaction with music. In fact, is many cases, it may have reduced the problem, at least during the time of interaction with music, thus alleviating the stress and "fear" aspects of the condition.

The one thing that music teachers and caregivers might keep in mind is that for children with auditory deficiencies, music is processed differently than in children without such deficits. The timbres (instrumental textures enabling discrimination of one instrument from another), certain tones (pitches that may not be perceived accurately), dynamics (volume), and most important, auditory figure-ground (separating particular foreground sound from background sounds and noise), can be problematic auditory issues. For instance, someone who has a cochlear implant tends to discriminate timbre in very limited ways; auditory issues that abound in ASD persons often produce an inability to determine important (central) sound from background, instead the listeners receive all sounds as if in a tsunami of sounds, rather than being able to focus on the important sound while eliminating others as "background."

These are just two examples that could exist in deficient auditory processing. These deficits can be treated through music therapy and music training since "ear training" and focused listening is a very pronounced training factor. Therefore instrumental learning could well be achieved with a music-based clinician who can teach and focus on ear training, as preliminary for a year or so, prior to resuming lessons with an instrumental instructor.

Should I consider earphones for my child?—Readers are surely aware that there are any number of opportunities and "therapies" that recommend the use of various types of earphones to assist a person with behavioral issues confronting auditory processing problems. Some earphones seem to eliminate various external sounds, and for some persons, may also assist with misophonia or hyperacusis (sensitive hearing), and other processing issues by "tuning out" extraneous acoustic stimuli. Other earphones tend to eliminate certain pitch frequencies that are deemed to be causing auditory discomforts. Still others simply shut out or reduce the level of volume (loudness) at concerts or other music activities, or in airplanes, malls, etc. Although the option of whether or not to apply earphones is up to the parent and/or clinician, I mostly do not recommend attempting to limit the intake of information by the auditory system—especially during a child's development. In short, earphones are Band-Aids, but do not lead to more permanent adaptation. Rather, I have observed that the more exposure to possibly discomforting sounds, the more *adaptive* the auditory system can become—especially in young children with much development still ahead. I prefer seating location considerations at concerts and classrooms, perhaps adapted instrumental positioning (if in private lessons), and general exposure to the seeming uncomfortable acoustic circumstances, because the brain *will* eventually develop a compensatory adaptation (coping) strategy.

One of my piano students, with perfect pitch, at first would become highly aroused by my out-of-tune piano, who, after several months of training on this out-of-tune piano, became so accustomed to the instrument being out of tune, he adapted, although always aware that the pitch was not accurate! (In other words, he didn't lose his perfect pitch, but learned to cope and accept that my instrument was not in perfect pitch.) In another case, I had an ASD student with perfect pitch who would demand music only if in the F-key on the piano, and CDs she enjoyed also were in the key of F. Still, in piano training, she was able, eventually, to tolerate other keys, especially the key of C, in which most beginner piano books are written. In time, this student became adept at modulating one song or another into the key of F. So if given a chance, adaptation will regulate arousal and behavior, without the need for earphones,

Visual
Visual impediments are a bit less intrusive in learning to play any instrument. For visually impaired students, the sense of touch becomes the prominent system, in conjunction with the auditory system, for aiding visual information processing. (Research has

indicated that despite the lack of vision, hearing and touch of items stimulate the occipital lobe, the vision-processing area of the brain, to light up, as if it were processing visual information.) Through the ages many talented individuals have become prominent and successful music professionals despite their visual impairment or complete blindness; for example, George Shearing, Moondog, José Feliciano, Art Tatum, Stevie Wonder, Ray Charles, Andrea Bocelli, to name just a few. Also, one can find lists of visually unabled ASD professional musicians, such as composer/performer Hikari Ōe, the non-verbal ASD son of the famous Nobel prize-winning Japanese author, Kenzaburō Ōe.[6]

Several resources for facilitating music instruction for visually impaired students are available, in Braille books, Braille music materials, and of course many apps now on computers. Several years ago I had the opportunity to volunteer at a Center for the Blind, that was undertaking a special project that transferred musical scores, by hand, into Bold Note Notation. *(Bold Note Notation is the enlargement of music notes onto the page, enabling visually impaired persons to read the music print in a larger, magnified version.)* In addition, I myself studied a bit of Braille and Braille music notation, which is very efficient in the teaching of instrumental and note-reading skills in a non-visual manner. Of course, there is always the imitation process through which the student hears the piece and finds the tones that replicate what s/he hears—a sort of rote-learning process. The tactile system's sense of touch discrimination plays an important role for students with impaired vision, so the input of a music therapist and an occupational therapist is very helpful in securing a well-functioning tactile system. In addition,

---

6   https://en.wikipedia.org/wiki/Hikari_%C5%8Ce

a music instructor with some knowledge of resources available to assist in teaching visually impaired students would be a plus. Adequate interaction between the auditory, visual, and tactile sensory systems is key in music training. The only deterrent to music skills learning would be the somewhat inaccurate information processing of these systems—a restraint, *but not an elimination!* Music is an equalizer. It does not discriminate between persons who "can" or "cannot" do. As repeated often throughout this book, music identifies *ability*, not *dis-*ability. There are few if any "deficiencies" in the presence of music. A skilled music therapist and/or instrumental instructor with experience in working with sensorimotor-impaired individuals can, indeed will, help the student become proficient and successful in music pursuits, at any ability level. The brain will change.

In his 1st grade class, my son's teacher discovered that he appeared to be dyslexic. She wondered how well he was reading piano music. I asked his piano teacher about that, and she said that when the music is upright on the keyboard or music stand, he is able to sequence information perfectly appropriately.

Dyslexia does not often show as a problem in reading music notation. Although this has never been officially researched, I suggested to this parent and others, that one reason could be related to the fact that reading notation is like looking at an art work—dots, lines, various symbols in a particular graphic sequence and design—flowing up, some down, pauses, etc. Perhaps reading written material—letter combinations written in a straight line across a page—is difficult to sequence, while dots, lines, shapes, and graphic designs are simpler? When this question came up with one of my piano students, I wrote the school teacher a note suggesting she try placing the words and letters in a more graphic arts design manner, with some letters up, some down, words and sentences flowing up and down, etc. Bingo! Suddenly the student did not seem to be constrained by dyslexic vision, and happily read the material without the need to invert words or letters. Of course this was only an experiment, but I believe that reading music is like observing a graphic "design" that can be different from just reading the letters on this page, printed in a straight line across the paper. How a book or paper is placed, for the comfort and benefit of the reader—both in school, and in the music lesson, has an impact on the readability of information with persons of dyslexic visual processing.

Another vision problem affecting many children, particularly children on the spectrum, is the problem of *scotopic sensitivity*. Known as *Irlen syndrome* (also referred to as *Meares-Irlen syndrome*, *scotopic sensitivity* syndrome, and visual stress), it is a perceptual visual-processing disorder. It is not an optical problem. It is a problem with the brain's ability to process visual information adequately. (This problem tends to run in families and is not currently identified by other standardized educational or medical tests.) Light sensitivity is a crucial disruption to persons with *scotopic sensitivity*, especially areas of light sensitivity involving glaring light reflections, fluorescent lights, sunlight or similar bright lights, and some night lights. Along with the sensitivity to light come physiological problems—feeling tired, dizziness, anxiety, irritability, headaches, restlessness, inability to remain focused—especially with bright or fluorescent lights.[7]

The importance of being aware of *scotopic sensitivity* is that paper glares and reflects light. When a book is lying flat on a desk, all overhead lights are reflected on the page (especially if the paper is highly glossy), and that tends to distort letters and written words. In addition, fluorescent lights so widely used in schools, tend, in addition to reflections, to emit an extremely high frequency sound that disturbs almost all students on the autism spectrum. School and music teachers should be made aware of this, in relation to any child, but especially for a child on the autism spectrum who already has various visual processing issues! Fortunately, music is placed upright, either on a piano or music stand, and although the material is printed on glossy paper, overheard light reflections and refractions of print are limited or less likely! So, taking the suggestion from music, reading materials and books should be in an upright reading position (as the cook places cook-books on a stand), at school, at a music lesson, at home, to reduce excess light stimulation.

Hyperarousal

Taking a child to hear music in live concerts is fully encouraged. Chapter 7 provides suggestions and advice on how to proceed and assist the child who is hyperactive, possibly hyperaroused, etc. Here I would like to remind parents that in some cases, music, which is auditory stimulation, may overwhelm the child's sensory

---

7   I recommend reading more information on Irlen syndrome at a site providing some detailed information: http://irlen.com/what-is-irlen-syndrome

systems, causing a hyperactive "melt-down." This problem may also rear its head when undertaking instrumental or vocal lessons. What to do? When choosing an instrument of study for the child (see Chapter 5), his or her reactions to the timbres and volume capacity of an instrument must be considered. The instrument of choice is the one preferred and chosen by the child, because of the likes or comforts of certain resonances. However, because I recommend piano as the first instrument, some initial resistance to piano lessons and "piano homework" (see Chapter 6) may be due to several auditory issues:

- child's perfect pitch creates discomfort with out-of-tune pianos, causing some behavior problems

- piano timbre may emit an overwhelming amount of resonance, overtones bouncing around a room, too loud/ soft uncontrolled volume

- too much auditory information at concerts may create habitual melt-downs at future events, to any type of "musical" sound, even outside of the concert hall

- auditory memory, visual tracking, and bilateral motor-planning may be more than the brain can tackle, thus inducing resistance behaviors

- location of the piano within a particular room, or near a wall, may cause extra reverberations along with some sensory/ visual discomfort

- figure-ground auditory focus, at home, at concerts, in the teacher's studio, where much ambient sounds emanate, would clearly cause arousals and fight-or-flight responses.

Many additional circumstances can hyperarouse the student, including likes or dislikes of particular songs, music registers (keys), or pitches, poor intonation in instructor's voice or instrument(s), and more.

Sometimes, hyperarousal at a concert or music lesson could result from non-music stimulation, but rather from previous or current conditions such as indigestion, argument with parent or sibling, elimination of favorite item such as a toy, decrease of computer or smartphone time, or other non-music-related issues causing anxieties that stimulate hyperarousal behavior problems erroneously attributed to the music experience. A child is a child! A child knows, instinctively, what will attract attention or reversal of action of a parent. A diagnosis does not eliminate the child's ability to be a child and to manipulate the parent verbally or behaviorally, in order to get what the child wants. Kids are kids, under any circumstances. The parent will be astute and knowledgeable of such things, able to keenly observe and assess the possible cause of the child's discomfort, and then determine the best course of action, without eliminating the music event. In the above section on auditory processing, I have a note about the use of earphones to reduce hyperarousal, that may provide some suggestions as to when, why, or why not, to apply earphones. I also discussed some visual issues that can cause anxiety states of behavior.

In sum, arousal, of any kind and anywhere, can come about for any number of reasons, some known, some unknown. Shutting sound or vision out or down may not be as effective as continuing within the acoustic or visual environment, with some natural adaptations, as a way of inducing adaptive conditioning to the real world of acoustic and visual stimulation. For scotopic sensitivity, one does not lower the lights continually, but rather, one takes adaptive measures to decrease discomfort, without having the person don dark glasses at any event! While the fully developed adult may require external implements for decreasing light and sound, a growing person is still in the developing stage that can still precipitate sensory adaptations. Yes, adjustment and coping may take some time, to the discomfort of the parent/caregiver/ teacher and other observers, but we are speaking of the growing child—the child's development and eventual comfort, and not a temporary Band-Aid for the comfort of the outsiders. There are many so-called "sensory-friendly" concerts and films—and that's fine, but they should not be exclusive of real-world, standard experiences, especially when auditory and visual discomforts are so diverse and misunderstood that it is difficult specifically to identify the precise problem in order to appease every participant! Too many "comforts" makes one become "comfortable" only in certain circumstances, while I would like any child, of any diagnosis, to learn to become comfortable in *any* circumstance, at any age, through gained adaptive processing. This is a less than popular point of view, subject to disagreement, so I leave it to the discretion of the reader to decide what is in the best developmental interest of their child(ren). In any event, music must continue!

CHAPTER 9

USEFUL INFORMATION AND HELPFUL RESOURCES

Music gives a soul to the universe, wings to the mind, flight to the imagination and life to everything.

PLATO

We come to the final chapter of this book, with a brief review, some resource recommendations, and some final notes to encouraging parents, caregivers, readers to seriously consider including music throughout the upbringing and development of the child. Every child, whether diagnosed or non-diagnosed benefits from music. As stated throughout, the brain functions better and becomes more efficient when influenced by the study of instrumental or vocal music. Here are some notes on how the human brain develops.

On brain development

In speaking of child development and music, and thinking beyond the spectrum when including music in a child's life, let us take a few moments to review some very basic information on brain development, in support of including music stimulation for developing good brain function, diagnosis notwithstanding! The brain begins to develop from the moment of conception, and continues in various stages throughout development, although not entirely in a consistent, predictable time frame and manner. Brain development *in utero* depends on many factors, including the mother's nutrition, the amount of in-utero fetal stimulation (including earphones to the belly during pregnancy), general health and care of the mother (e.g., relaxed or anxious, hurried or slowed, etc.). In other words, *everything* that happens outside of the womb influences what occurs within. One timeline suggests that some three or four weeks after conception, a thin layer of cells that forms on the embryo begins to fold and fuse, structuring something akin to a liquid tube. This becomes the basis of the brain and spinal cord. Within this first month, cells in this tube begin to multiply profusely, ultimately creating some 250,000 or more neurons per minute! In fact, most of the brain's lifetime of cells—I repeat, *lifetime of cells*—are produced by the end of six months in the womb! At about the third month (14 weeks or so), some cells begin to perform some elementary physiological functions, and the majority of cells begin to lodge into various regions throughout the still-forming brain. This point is often when some "brain mistakes" can happen, when cells might lodge in the wrong place, ultimately producing incorrect processes that later become diagnosable as various disorders (e.g., psychiatric disorders, developmental and language delays, etc.). By the fifth or sixth month of pregnancy, the brain will have shed most of its unused cells (about half of those originally produced), with the remaining cells now distributed and organized into over 40 different regions that eventually will result in sensory, emotional, cognitive, and physiological processes (muscles, language, vision, etc.).

By the time the fetus becomes a fully formed newborn entering the planet nine months later, the brain has developed some *100-billion neurons* (cells)! But these neurons need to be activated through endless forms of internal and external stimulation, in order to become efficient. By the age of three, developmental milestones become part of neuronal interactions geared toward survival behaviors. As brain structures develop, the infant begins to reach, point, grasp at will, turn over, recognize familiar persons, discriminate between parent and others, crawl, stand, walk, talk, etc. In early years (three to eight years of age), the brain has established many connections and pathways, based on the many *repetitions* of actions, experiences, stimulations, many of which will become permanent.

From the age of ten forward until late adolescence, the brain begins to discard (prune) some early-formed connections, which are now insufficient, inefficient, and weak. Connections that have been somehow neglected or used infrequently are now permanently discarded. By the time the child reaches 18 years of age, brain neurons have been reduced to basically the same amount that the young child had at the age of eight months old! By 18, brain adaptation is also less strong, although it can still take place because the brain, by adulthood, is quite powerful, strong, and always plastic. By adulthood, brain structures have expanded and given rise to "the mind," emotions, cognitive thoughts, the ability to communicate in one way or another, and to undertake necessary survival maneuvers (fight-flight, etc.). These are survival instincts that are reinforced through stimulation of various kinds (education, music, art, etc.).

This quick summary of information about brain development is precisely why I join scientists in recommending *music from the start of life*, with music participation and instruction at least by age three or four, to continue throughout life, because the more positive and *repetitive* organized stimulation the brain receives, the better and more efficient is the development of neurons and neuronal interactions for information processing and functional adaptation. As it is said, "the brain is a continuous work in progress," with neurons formed, deleted, transferred, and taught to conduct various actions throughout one's life. Therefore, the term "brain plasticity" supports the possibility of redirecting and altering various developmental diagnoses and maladaptive responses for any and every child![8]

Every stimulus changes the brain. And music, one of few activities that is a whole-brain, whole-body stimulus, activates multiple brain areas, developing new neuronal connections in multiple areas. Language is not necessary for music interaction. Understanding music is not necessary in order for music to impact upon the human system. Emotions are immediately sensitized. Feelings, aesthetic sensations, are felt throughout one's body—whether or not the person is aware of this. *Ah...,* you say, *my child does not function on a higher cognitive level. My child is said to be unteachable, and that he will not benefit from any kind of music activity.* Of course, that is absurd. Music benefits even a comatose person! Vibrations massage the body, tonalities soothe, and active playing of an instrument—however minimally—stimulates movement, motor sensations, and an awareness of self. And there is the voice providing vibrations within one's own body. The kazoo, into which one hums to derive a buzzing tone, provides oral motor stimulation through sensed vibrations. Blowing a recorder regulates breathing. What? Your child does not blow? Given enough time, s/he will learn to blow,

---

8   Source and further information: www.ag.ndsu.edu/pubs

because the brain receives tonality that further stimulates the desire for repetition!

Music therapy resources

Music therapy was discussed in a previous chapter. Many caregivers, teachers, parents are not fully aware of this form of clinical treatment. If a child is a bit less able or ready to undertake full instrumental learning, I recommend beginning with music-based clinical work that could include some instrumental training, as discussed in previous chapters. Below is a list of Associations around the world, through which one can obtain information on procuring a music-based clinician. Some contact links are not provided, but readers can surely undertake internet searches for obtaining current contact information, This information is provided courtesy of the World Federation of Music Therapy.[9]

North America

American Music Therapy Association: www.musictherapy.org

Canadian Association for Music Therapy: www.musictherapy.ca

Certification Board for Music Therapists www.cbmt.org

Australia/New Zealand

Australian Music Therapy Association: www.austmta.org.au

Music Therapy New Zealand: www.musictherapy.org.nz

---

9   www.musictherapyworld.net/WFMT/Home.html

Southeast Asia

Indian Association of Music Therapy: http://iamt.net.in

South Africa

South African Music Therapy Association: www.samta.co.za

Western Pacific

Chinese Professional Music Therapist Association: www.chinamusictherapy.org

Hong Kong Music Therapy Association: www.musictherapyhk.org

Japanese Music Therapy Association: www.jmta.jp

Korean Music Therapy Association: www.musictherapy.or.kr

Association for Music Therapy Singapore: www.singaporemusictherapy.wordpress.com

Music Therapy Association of Taiwan: www.musictherapy.org.tw

Eastern Mediterranean

None

Latin America

Asociación Argentina de Musicoterapia: www.musicoterapia.org.ar

União Brasileira das Associações de Musicoterapia: www.musicoterapia.mus.br

Asociación Chilena de Musicoterapia: www.achim.cl

Asociación Colombiana de Musicoterapia: Email alcomut@
hotmail.com

Asociación de Musicoterapeutas Cubanos : Email teruquilinda3@
yahoo.com.mx; teresaf@colef.mx; olga@cubarte.cult.cu

Instituto Mexicano de Musicoterapia Humanista:
www.musicoterapias.com

Europe

Austrian Association websites:

—ÖBM: www.oebm.org

—Viennese Institute of Music Therapy:
www.wim-musiktherapie.at

—Institute for Ethno-Music Therapy: www.ethnomusik.com

—Professional Association of Ethno Music Therapy:
www.bfem.at

British Association for Music Therapy: www.bamt.org

Czech Republic Association websites:

—International Association of Art Therapies: www.maut.cz

—Music Therapy Association of the Czech Republic:
www.musictherapy.cz

Danish Music Therapy Association: www.musikterapi.org

Dutch Association for Music Therapy: www.nvvmt.nl

Estonian Music Therapy Society: www.muusikateraapia.eu

(Germany) Federal Association of Music Therapy:
www.bag-musiktherapie.de

(Greece) Hellenic Association of Certified Professional Music
Therapists: www.musictherapy.gr

Irish Association of Creative Arts Therapists:
www.iacat.ie

Association of Polish Music Therapists:
www.muzykoterapiapolska.pl

Dalcroze Eurhythmics resources

The suggestion that eurhythmics movement, based on the work of
Emile Jaques-Dalcroze, be included in training, was discussed in
Chapter 4. Here I encourage music training to include eurhythmics
movement for developing good rhythmic body and mind coordination
along with the study of an instrument. In my book *Eurhythmics
for Autism and Other Neurophysiologic Diagnoses: A Sensorimotor
Music-Based Clinical Approach* (2015, Jessica Kingsley Publishers),
I detail physiological and sensorimotor information, and describe
how eurhythmics adapted in music-based clinical work has been
extremely beneficial to participants on the autism spectrum
and others. I continue to urge parents, teachers, caretakers to
include eurhythmics for kids 'n' music. Further information may
be obtained from various international Dalcroze sources; several
are listed here:

Dalcroze Society of America

www.dalcrozeusa.org

International Federation of Eurhythmics Teachers (FIER)
www.fier.com

Jacques-Dalcroze Institute, Geneva, Switzerland
www.dalcroze.ch

Dalcroze Canada
www.dalcrozecanada.com

Dalcroze Australia
www.dalcroze.org.au

Dalcroze UK
www.dalcroze.org.uk

Italian Jaques-Dalcroze Association
www.dalcroze.it

Dalcroze Society of Taiwan
http://blog.roodo.com/dalcroze

Dalcroze Society of Japan
www.j-dalcroze-society.com

Dalcroze class in Mexico
www.musicaviva.com.mx

If your country is not listed, you might contact the Jacques-Dalcroze Institute in Geneva, Switzerland, for additional information.

To find instrumental and other music lessons, as stated previously, local music conservatories, schools of music, universities, and school music teachers can provide excellent referral information. In addition, parent support groups often have local information on music training persons and organizations. Schools also can lead parents to business concerns that handle instrumental sales, music training materials, kazoos, recorders, drum mallets, and a variety of other needs. Such concerns also provide music lessons or participating instructors.

For home music activities there are a myriad of books, games, musical toys, song books, and a brief search through the internet, or at schools and music stores, will provide an infinite supply of sources and obtainable materials. One caution: Do not purchase "toy" musical instruments, since there may be intonation problems, and the toys may not last very long. Furthermore, if possible, stay away from plastic toys, other than recorders and kazoos, which are best in plastics since these can be washed. Drums should be made of natural skins rather than plastic heads, where possible and financially convenient. All other tonal instruments and keyboards should be real instruments—*not* toys! If possible, we as parents and caregivers would like to help the auditory, visual, and tactile systems to learn correct information from the start. Real xylophones are better than toys, which often are not in correct tune.

CADENCE

It is hoped that pertinent questions have been covered throughout the chapters of this book. My objective in writing this book will be fulfilled if the reader remembers several important concepts I have attempted to share.

A diagnosis does not pre-empt ability or skill! We are all equal in the music environment. There is no right or wrong to music interaction. Some persons may be more successful than others, some may attain skills sooner than others, some may never attain adequate skills. These eventualities do not limit a child's interaction in the music realm. All brains benefit from music.

From birth and throughout life, music should be part of the life of all children, of any ability, typical or diagnosed! Music brings better quality of life to everyone. Some exceptional attitudes on the part of parents and caretakers may be required, but "expectations," other than the reward of music and brain development, should be carefully determined based on the reality of potential achievements.

If talent and excellent skills are evident in the child of any diagnosis, as well as a typically functioning child, proceed to a possible professional life in music! Music vs. sports is not a decision. Music and sports can coexist. And if a child's musical interest excels, fear not that s/he will "starve as a musician." Anyone can starve, in any profession and skill! The criteria are happiness and contentment—not necessarily financial rewards and recognition.

Finally, *"Kids 'n' Music" means thinking beyond the spectrum*, and ensuring that music is part of his or her life, throughout life. To quote philosopher Friedrich Nietzsche: "Without music, life would be a mistake."

See to it that your child's life will never be a mistake!

FINALE

Music gives a soul to the universe, wings to the mind, flight to the imagination and life to everything.

PLATO

I bring this book to a close as Chapter 1 opened, with a quote by Plato. There are many who confirm the importance of music in child development and growth, especially in children diagnosed on the autism spectrum, and other functional deficits. The information within this book is just a brief reminder of what we often take for granted—that the *best* way to reach a child, and a special needs child, is *not* through words or numbers or directives, but through the *emotions*. Emotions drive behaviors. Behaviors communicate needs. Behaviors can be redirected, not with words and commands, but with simple songs, musical interactions, and the joy of making music.

Certainly many areas related to special-needs *kids 'n' music* have been left un-discussed. A spectrum is, after all, a *spectrum* as wide and varied as are human beings. Music does not divide but rather, *unites* the varieties into one, total experience, equally comprehended and appreciated by any human being. I end the book with the following quote:

The power of music to integrate and cure...is quite fundamental. It is the profoundest nonchemical medication.

OLIVER SACKS